To the peoples of the world who broke through barriers of colour, race and creed to unite in the preservation for posterity of this magnificent treasure.

◀ *Overleaf*. Legs of colossal statue of Ramses II, later usurped by Pinodjem, high priest of Amun. Ramses' Queen stands between his knees.   *Temple of Karnak, Luxor.*

Near Abu Simbel the rising waters threaten a village behind the palms.   ▶

Overleaf, facing title page. The stairs leading down to the burial chamber in the tomb of Queen Nefertary. ▶ The Queen is offering wine to Isis, behind whom sits Nephthys. In the angle the figure of Maet spreads her wings. The atmosphere is feminine and there is no feeling of gloom or death.

Mummified head of Ramses II.

ABU
SIMBEL

WILLIAM MacQUITTY

Foreword by Dr. I. E. S. Edwards

MACDONALD : LONDON

FIRST PUBLISHED IN 1965 BY
MACDONALD & CO. (PUBLISHERS) LTD.
GULF HOUSE, 2 PORTMAN STREET, LONDON, W.1
MADE AND PRINTED IN GREAT BRITAIN BY
PURNELL & SONS, LTD.
PAULTON (SOM.) AND LONDON

FOREWORD

by Dr. I. E. S. Edwards, *Keeper of Egyptian Antiquities, The British Museum*

Nearly ninety years ago Amelia Edwards, in *A Thousand Miles Up the Nile*, wrote of Ramses II: "We seem to know the man—to feel his presence—to hear his name in the air," and yet she felt compelled, in the end, to admit that any attempt to clothe his monuments with a sketch of his personality would be "a mere exercise of fancy". Since those romantic days, when travel in Egypt was a gay adventure, much has been learnt about the ancient Pharaohs, but most of them still remain as inscrutable as the statues and sculptures in relief which they placed in their temples. Many of their subjects, unhampered by the shackles of royal protocol, have left a far clearer image of themselves, sometimes as a result of the chance preservation of documents mentioning incidents in their lives which were never intended to survive as memorials. Only rarely is a corner of the veil lifted in the case of kings, so that we can think of them as individuals differing in character from those who preceded and followed them. Ramses II is undoubtedly one of these exceptions. It is true that what he tells us in his inscriptions is patently tendentious; it is exclusively what he wanted us to know. Even when he confesses that he was duped by a couple of Bedouin before the battle of Kadesh his intention was not to reveal his credulity or to call attention to his trusting disposition but to add to the glory of his ultimate triumph. If he possessed finer qualities than we can detect in his official records our chances of discovering their nature are slender. To us his outstanding characteristics must remain his vanity and unbounded arrogance, the urge to win immortality at any cost. His method lacked subtlety; it was the technique of effect by mass and frequent repetition. From the Dog River in the Lebanon to far south in the Sudan the traveller could not fail to notice his monuments. He was, moreover, completely unscrupulous, thinking nothing of superimposing his name on the works of his predecessors, and, on occasion, usurping them completely.

With the emphasis mainly on quantity, it is not surprising that much of the sculpture of the time lacks any aesthetic appeal and originality. No single generation could have produced enough artistic talent to meet such a demand. Paradoxically, however, we owe to Ramses II and his contemporaries one of the outstanding architectural achievements of antiquity, namely the massive rock temples of Abu Simbel. In conception, moreover, their external design was something entirely new. Opinions on the artistic qualities of the façades differ widely, but their impressiveness cannot be denied. No one with an eye for dramatic effect who has had the good fortune to sail up the Nile and has seen the king's temple gradually emerging through the haze of an early summer morning can have remained unmoved by the experience. Largely because of the flatness of the Nile valley most of the surviving temples, with the notable exception of Deir el-Bahri, seem to have no environmental *raison d'être*; there is nothing to suggest that nature intended them to be there. Not so with the temples of Abu Simbel, where the setting is perfect, and the monuments are to scale with their surroundings. Herein lies the real tragedy of the present situation. Given the necessary funds, the fabric can be saved from destruction, but the setting will be lost for ever. Future generations must depend very largely for their appreciation of these monuments on the results of the photographic skill of their predecessors, among whom it is safe to predict that the author of this book will occupy a place of honour.

A mere decade ago few travellers, even Egyptologists, visited the temples of

Abu Simbel, but their impending destruction has brought tourists from all over the world to see them, and every schoolboy knows the name of the king for whom they were constructed. Little could Ramses II have imagined that, for a brief spell at least, three thousand years after his death his fame would spread far beyond the limits of the empire over which he ruled as a god incarnate. We owe it chiefly to him that the last five years have seen the greatest concentration of archaeological effort in history. Without the appeal to the imagination made by the prospect of losing Abu Simbel it is most unlikely that much of the support which has been given to the Nubian campaign of rescue would have been forthcoming. Great Britain alone has contributed more than £150,000 towards the cost of salvage, not to mention giving an immense amount of scientific help. In all, some seventeen nations have responded to the appeal of Unesco by sending expeditions to the doomed area, and everything humanly possible has been done to make sure that its archaeological legacy will be preserved for posterity. Rather ironically, however, little fresh information about Ramses II has come to light, whereas many of the kings whose memory he tried to suppress in his lifetime have gained appreciably in stature. But nothing can detract from the renown of Ramses II or rob the temples of Abu Simbel of the unique position which they occupy in the architectural history of ancient Egypt. Those who read the factual, but none the less fascinating, story as related in this book and study the many beautiful photographs will surely feel, like Amelia Edwards, that they "know the man". They will also learn something about the efforts which have been made to preserve the temples from complete destruction. Lastly they will appreciate what the building of the High Dam will mean to the population of Egypt in terms of economic and agricultural gain.

I. E. S. Edwards.

CONTENTS

ACKNOWLEDGMENTS

I wish to thank the many members of the following organisations who gave so willingly of their time and counsel for their help and kindness during the research and writing of this book: UNESCO representatives in Paris and in Cairo, H. E. Dr. Abdul Kader Hatem, Deputy Prime Minister for Culture and National Guidance in the U.A.R., Egyptian Department of Antiquities, Centre de Documentation sur l'Ancienne Egypte, the Cairo Museum, the U.A.R. Information Centre, London, the Egyptian Department of the British Museum whose Keeper, Dr. I. E. S. Edwards, most kindly wrote the Foreword and checked the manuscript, Ove Arup and Partners, Consulting Engineers, Fry, Drew and Partners, Architects, who kindly helped the author with his plan for Abu Simbel, and J. D. M. Harvey, who did the sketches for the appendix.

Several quotations are made in the text and the publishers wish to thank the following for permission to use them: the Griffith Institute for permission to quote from *The Kadesh Inscriptions of Ramses II* by Sir Alan Gardiner (1960); Hutchinson & Company (Publishers) Limited for permission to quote from *Ancient Egyptian Religion* by J. Černý (1952); the Clarendon Press for permission to quote from *Egypt of the Pharaohs* by Sir Alan Gardiner (1964); and the British Academy for permission to quote from *Comparative Study of the Literatures of Egypt, Palestine and Mesopotamia* by T. E. Peet (1929).

Technical Data. I used two Asahi Pentax cameras, models S3 and SV, each fitted with the Asahi Pentax CdS clip-on exposure meters. One was loaded with Kodak Tri-X black and white film and the other either with Kodachrome II or Kodak High Speed Ektachrome film. Sometimes both cameras were loaded with colour film. I used three Asahi Pentax lenses: Takumar 1.8, 55 mm; Auto-Takumar 3.5, 35 mm; Super-Takumar 3.5, 135 mm. I also carried two electronic flash guns and plastic bags to protect the equipment from dust. I usually shot at $\frac{1}{125}$th of a second, working to the meter reading for aperture.

1: THE STORY OF ABU SIMBEL

The story of Abu Simbel began when the world began. During the Cretaceous period 135 million years ago great layers of sandstone were deposited near what is now known as Wadi Halfa on the borders of Egypt and the Sudan. Some of these layers were compact and hard, others were soft and crumbly. For millions of years the fast-flowing waters of the Nile eroded a channel through the sandstone, forming high cliffs. In these cliffs the hard layers were exposed reddish-brown against the golden biscuit of the softer stone. The deeper colour was caused by the presence of iron in the form of ferruginous cement. At this point in its course the great river curves, forming a delightful bay. Here the milky green water laps at tall sandstone cliffs over 300 feet high. Such an imposing position is rare in the arid desert through which the river flows. Ramses II (1304–1237 B.C.) did not have to look further for the site for his great temple at Abu Simbel and work was begun on the building about 1270 B.C.

His Egyptian masons were quick to make use of the natural advantage that the sandstone offered. The hard layers formed ceilings, supported by their own compactness. Vertical fissures simplified the excavating of the huge shelf from which the figures thrust outwards and upwards. The Ancient Egyptians were masters in

◀ Façade of the temple of Queen Nefertary. In the recesses are four colossal statues of Ramses II. A frieze of sacred cobras guards the entrance. Below them is a scene of the king offering wine to Amen-Re and to Horus. On both sides of the doorway are carved his name and titles.   *Abu Simbel.*

Granite ushabti-figure of King Taharqa of the Ethiopian XXVth Dynasty (c. 689–664 B.C.). Ushabti-figures were placed in tombs in large numbers. The inscription written upon them was one of the spells from the Book of the Dead instructing them that, when the god called upon their owner to work in the Hereafter, they were to answer for him and say, "Here am I", and to perform the task required. (See page 86.)

the handling of stone. They loved and understood it, and even with the crude tools of the period they were able to get results which by modern standards would be regarded as superb. The entrance to the temple was contrived so that the first rays of the rising sun shone directly on it. Following this line, the masons quarried more than 180 feet into the rock, always in line with the sun. Today the innermost chamber is lit by the golden rays just as it was when it was first excavated. The site was unique, but why did Ramses build the rock temple at Abu Simbel in a place so remote that it lay undiscovered until 1812? To find the answer we must go back to the beginning of man's existence in the Valley of the Nile.

Little is known of the first inhabitants of this area. In their day, more than five thousand years ago, there was heavy rainfall and the moist atmosphere destroyed all traces of their life except for a few flint implements and weapons. Today only deep ravines remain to show the course of the torrents which then helped to swell the waters of the Nile. Gradually, the dry desert prevailed and the changed climate faithfully preserved the astonishing history of the later inhabitants.

The desert is rich in history—dig almost at random and some trace of the past is revealed. The earliest burials discovered were simple. The body lay on its side in a flexed position, hands frequently placed over the eyes. Below it, a mat of rushes, above more rushes and then the dry preserving sand. The bodies were desiccated, not mummified, but sometimes the flesh was removed from the skeleton, as is done in Thailand today. Sometimes the bodies were smoked, as they are now in Papua. It was clear that value was set upon preservation—some form of continued life after death was sought. Beside the body were pots for food and drink and weapons and implements to assist the owner in a new existence.

Life and death were constantly in the thoughts of the Egyptians. Egypt is a country of sharp contrasts. The yellow sand of the desert marches beside the rich green pastures growing in the black-red soil deposited by the flooding Nile. The receding waters leave a clear division: black for life, yellow for death. The all-pervading dryness preserves every dead creature until the living devour it. Overhead the fiery sun rides across the clear sky only to vanish in a blaze of glory in the sunset of the Western Desert. At night the sun enters the Underworld, where all mankind goes after death. In the morning it rises again to make once more its triumphant journey across the Heavens. Egypt is a land of sun; for the Egyptians it was a god. Perhaps this accounts for the crouching dead with their hands before their eyes to protect them from the blinding light of the god. Many of the bodies are buried facing west, where their future waited.

Later, as belief in life in another world became more general, burials became more complex. Unfortunately, early attempts to protect the dead body failed. The roughly-built graves prevented the hot, dry sand from reaching the body and desiccating it and, to the dismay of the tribe, the protected corpse disintegrated in natural decay. This led eventually, as we shall see, to elaborate forms of embalming, but an immediate remedy consisted in covering the body with a great earthenware bowl which, while protecting it from wild animals, still allowed the hot sand to do its work. In the grave were pots for food and drink, models of boats and wattle huts, with toys and games like ninepins for the children. The older girls were not forgotten—carved palettes for grinding green malachite to make eye-shadow link them with their sisters of today. Later, these palettes were carved with scenes depicting the great deeds of the time, a dual aspect which has been of great service to historians.

The people living in Egypt at this time, according to Professor Petrie, consisted of five distinct elements, the main one being the white-skinned Libyan tribes of North Africa, possibly of European origin, and the black-skinned African tribes such as the Somalis and Gallas. These were joined by a nomadic people of Semitic origin and were completely absorbed by the existing race, although traces of their language are in evidence.

These different tribes gradually formed two kingdoms: one of the Upper Nile, White, and one of the Lower Nile or Delta, Red. The earliest records show these kingdoms at war with one another. In the Chronological Table you will see that

Predynastic burial of a man from Gebelein. Mummification was not practised at this time; the corpse has entirely dried out in the hot sand so that the skin and hair have remained intact. Pottery and flints, the household belongings of this man, were buried with him.　　　　　　　　　　　　3100 B.C. *British Museum.*

King Menes, the first of the dynastic rulers, succeeded in uniting the two kingdoms, and from this point history is less conjectural, although it must be remembered that there is much more unknown than known of the history of these extraordinary people. Perhaps future excavations will help to provide the missing information, but then only to a limited degree. Most of the records that have survived have been found in the brick or stone-built tombs and were more concerned with the after-life than the daily existence of the people. None of the houses which at one

19

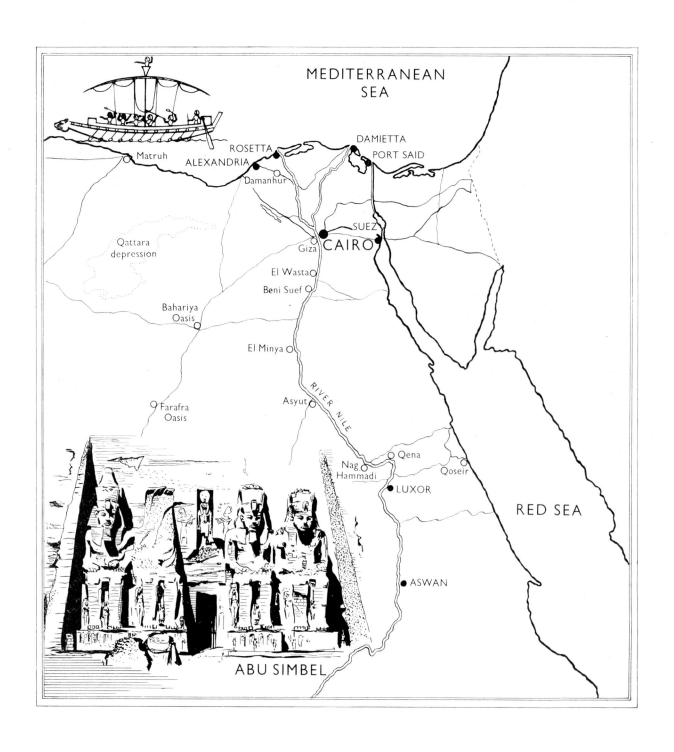

MEDITERRANEAN
SEA

Matruh
ROSETTA
ALEXANDRIA
DAMIETTA
PORT SAID
Damanhur
Qattara
depression
SUEZ
Giza CAIRO
El Wasta
Beni Suef
Bahariya
Oasis
El Minya
Farafra
Oasis
Asyut
RIVER NILE
Qena
Nag.
Hammadi
Qoseir
LUXOR
RED SEA
ASWAN

ABU SIMBEL

Book of the Dead of the Scribe Ani. Judgement scene; weighing the heart of Ani. The jackal-headed god, Anubis, tends the scales in which the heart (conscience) of Ani is weighed against the feather of Truth. Both must be of equal weight. The soul of Ani, represented as a human-headed bird, stands on top of his tomb which is painted white. *XVIIIth Dynasty, c.* 1400 B.C. *British Museum.*

time provided homes for the priests and slaves of the great temple of Abu Simbel remains. Only the dead and their preoccupation with their innumerable deities survive.

The civilisation of Ancient Egypt advances rapidly from this point. During the First Dynasty there were offices for the Royal Seal Bearer, the Royal Architect, the Keeper of the King's Vineyards and a Commander of the Inundation. The

21

The great pylon at Karnak, showing the remains of the ramp of earth up which the blocks of stone were hauled. The same principle was used to build the pyramids.

Book of the Dead of the Scribe Ani. Isis and Nephthys kneel upon the sign for gold on either side of a *djed*-column. The *ankh*, sign of life, supports in its human arms the sun's disc, which six baboons with upraised paws are worshipping. No doubt, similar baboons watched for the dawn at Abu Simbel.

XVIIIth Dynasty, c. 1400 B.C. *British Museum.*

A deserted Nubian village, soon to be engulfed by the rising waters. The palm trees in the foreground have already been partly covered.

regulating of the flooding of the Nile was as important then as today. Even with the modern immensity of the High Dam the principle is unchanged. In spring the melting snows on the mountains of Central Africa and the heavy rains which fall in the lake districts of the Equator start rivulets, growing into torrents which come down in spate through Ethiopia. This water is held by a series of dams in the Sudan and Upper Egypt until it is high enough to spread in a shallow sea over the arable land of Egypt. Here it deposits the rich mud which it has carried on its long journey. In this manner every year, about mid-July, the flood begins. By September the waters start to subside. There may be a flush in October but by December the river returns to its normal level.

The success of the inundation depends on the ability of the farmers and controllers to flood as large an area as possible with the correct amount of life-giving muddy water. Too much is wasteful; too little will not permit the crops to grow. From

Book of the Dead of the Scribe Ani. Ani and his wife, Tutu, are worshipping. Tutu holds in her hands a sistrum and a necklace with a long pendant which hangs down her back to balance the weight of the collar. On her head is a lotus flower and a cone of perfume. In front of them is a table of offerings piled with fruit, vegetables and bread.   *XVIIIth Dynasty, c.* 1400 B.C. *British Museum.*

the great flooding river out to the poorest farmer of the desert fringe, all must play their part in the delicate balance of irrigation. As the water flows farther away from the Nile the dams and sluices become smaller and smaller. Eventually, a spadeful of earth is sufficient to direct it from one channel to another in the plots of the small cultivators. The administration of such a complex operation reveals the high standard of government and control exercised by the early Egyptians. Apart from supplying fertility to this parched land, the Nile also indicated the rate of taxes that

General view of part of the papyrus.

would be levied on the people. This was calculated by the height of the flood—the higher the flood, the more harvest and the greater the tax.

With the passage of time, burial customs became more sophisticated and complex. Bodies were no longer placed in the ground—at least, not the bodies of the famous. Elaborate chambers, sometimes of great size, protected the beautifully-carved stone coffins in which the Pharaohs lay. Concealed entrances, sliding tapering doors and mountains of stone were used to hide the sacred corpses from tomb

27

Book of the Dead of the Scribe Ani. Amemit, composed of a crocodile, a leopard and a hippopotamus, waits to devour the deceased if the weighing goes against him.   *XVIIIth Dynasty, c.* 1400 B.C. *(detail of page* 27).

Mummy mask of Amenophis I. The mask is made of wood and the eyes and eyebrows are inlaid with glass. The dried, plaited garlands were probably placed over the coffin by the priests who, in the XXIst Dynasty (c. 1000 B.C.), reburied the mummies of many kings whose tombs had been plundered.
Early XVIIIth Dynasty, c. 1546–1526 B.C. *Cairo Museum.*

Overleaf, left. Female musicians playing harp, lute and flute. On their heads they have cones of perfumed oil.
Tomb of Nakht (see page 38).

Overleaf, right. Female attendants, probably daughters of Menna. One holds a bunch of papyrus stems and vase. They both wear heavy wigs and large gold earrings.   *Tomb of Menna (see page* 40).

robbers. Although the later tombs were constructed below the ground or tunnelled into limestone cliffs, the early ones were built above ground level. The first of these immense stone buildings to survive to the present day is the step pyramid of Saqqara. It was built by Imhotep for King Zoser and consists of five mastabas, rectangular box formations of stone, placed one on top of the other in the shape of a pyramid. The base is 396 feet by 352 feet and the height 195 feet. The chambers and passages underneath were lined with blue and green glazed tiles and bore the name of the king. This was the forerunner of the great pyramid of Cheops, the sole remaining wonder of the world and still the largest man-made building. When built it measured 755 feet square at the base and rose to a height of 481 feet.

This tremendous undertaking shows quite clearly the absolute power of the Pharaohs. It is calculated that the operation took a hundred thousand men twenty years to complete. The ramp up which the heavy blocks were dragged on sledges took ten years to build. The weight of the mass is about six million tons and the area it covers is more than thirteen acres.

Ramses offering lettuces (an aphrodisiac) to Min — interior Great Temple of Abu Simbel.

Nakht, Scribe and Astronomer of Amun, and his wife. The collars they wear are made of many faience (glazed composition) beads. Nakht has plain cylindrical beads, his wife's are in imitation of flower petals and fruit. Her collar may even be glazed inlay in gold. Tomb of Nakht. *Thebes (Luxor). XVIIIth Dynasty, c.1420 B.C.*

More remarkable than the immense size of the pyramid is the fine quality of the work. The dressing of the huge blocks is so accurate that a lubricating film of cement scarcely thicker than this page was sufficient to slide them together. Inside the pyramid the work is of the same excellence; the entrance passage joints are almost impossible to locate. Finally, when the king had been placed in the burial chamber and the entrance sealed with a tapering stone slab, no trace of an entrance could have been visible. In spite of all these precautions, the granite sarcophagus no longer contains the body of the king, nor has it ever been traced

Anubis, god of embalmment, holding the mummy of Ameniryirt. Painted wood.
XXVth Dynasty, c. 700 B.C.   *British Museum.*

Wooden sarcophagus of a cat,
painted white and green.
British Museum.

Mummies of cats sacred to the
goddess Bastet of Bubastis in the
Delta.   *British Museum.*

35

Painted wooden model of a man ploughing. He pressed the plough, which probably had a metal share, into the ground while the oxen dragged it along. This method of ploughing was used throughout Egyptian history, and is still in use. *XIIth Dynasty, c. 1800 B.C. British Museum.*

since. The limestone sheath which once entirely covered the pyramid has also vanished, looted to provide stone for later buildings.

Nearby is the Sphinx—the most famous of Egyptian sculptures. Like the sculptures of Abu Simbel, this is also carved from the living rock and, like Abu Simbel, is probably a royal portrait.

The jewels and gold adorning the mummies of the Pharaohs were a natural

Son and daughter of Menna presenting offerings of wine, milk and lotus flowers in his tomb.
Tomb of Menna (see page 40).

Men loading the wheat they have cut into a basket which they will carry between them on a pole. A girl bending down is gleaning ears of corn and the woman the other side of the picture is picking flax.   *Tomb of Nakht.*

target for tomb robbers. So adept did the robbers become that only one tomb has been discovered nearly intact—that of Tutankhamen. He was only a boy of eighteen and relatively unimportant, but the wealth that surrounded his mummy startled the world when it was discovered and still draws people from every country to gaze upon it in the Cairo Museum.

Occasionally the tomb robbers were caught, and an account of the robbery of the tomb of King Sebek-em-Saf is recorded by the commissioners in the Twentieth Dynasty. The robbers revealed under torture how they had undermined the king's

◀ Five men treading grapes in a stone vat: they hold on to ropes hanging from the crossbeam in order to steady themselves among the heady vapours. The sixth man watches the juice pouring into another vat. *Above:* jars already stoppered with clay seals. *Tomb of Nakht, Scribe and Astronomer of Amun, Luxor. XVIIIth Dynasty, c.* 1420 B.C. The tombs of the courtiers of the XVIIIth Dynasty were situated on the other side of the hill from the Valley of the Kings.

Menna, Scribe of the Fields of the Lord of the Two Lands of Upper and Lower Egypt, hunting birds in the papyrus marshes. He is accompanied by his wife, who steadies him as he hurls his throwing stick, and daughters, who hold the catch and pull up lotus flowers from the water for him.

Royal tombs were not decorated with scenes of everyday life and it is only from the private tombs that we can learn anything about the pleasures of the court and the non-warlike activities of the king.

Tomb of Menna, Luxor. XVIIIth Dynasty, c. 1420 B.C.

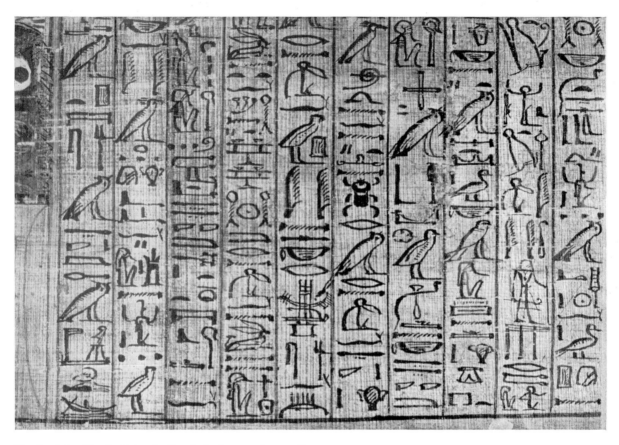

Book of the Dead of the Scribe Ani. Incomplete spells.

tomb from an adjacent chamber (rather in the manner of bank thieves today). The confession reads: "We found the august mummy of the king with his divine axe beside him and many amulets and ornaments of gold about his neck. His head was overlaid above with gold; his coffins were burnished with gold and silver, within and without, and inlaid with all kinds of stones."

The problem of tomb robbing continued, unabated by any punishments that the Pharaohs and priests could devise. Ramses II must have been well aware of the danger and obviously he took great care over the concealment of his tomb, which almost certainly contained infinitely more valuable treasure than that of the boy

Stone coffins recovered from the cache of royal mummies found in the tomb of Queen Inhapi at Deir-el-Bahri. Perhaps Ramses lay in one of these before being moved to Cairo Museum in 1886.

Pharaoh, Tutankhamen. Alas, he fared no better than the others. The new places of concealment were soon known to the tomb robbers; perhaps they were kept informed by dishonest priests. Fortunately, a dispute between two brother robbers led to the discovery in 1881 of a cache of some thirty royal mummies, including Ramses II. These are now safely housed in the Cairo Museum. Although the loss of the mummy was a serious matter, the practical Egyptians had provided for the possibility of loss or of disintegration through the ravages of time. For this purpose figures of the dead Pharaoh were placed in the mortuary temple. These were lifelike representations of the originals and would provide a resting place for the "ka" or vital force of the Pharaoh. Great importance was attached to the "ka" recognising its habitation—and the statues were therefore given the most realistic treatment. Whilst statues in the round were treated in normal perspective, those in bas-relief were usually shown from different viewpoints: the head in profile, the chest front view,

◀ Book of the Dead of the Scribe Ani. Incomplete spells.

43

and the rest of the body viewed from the side, farther arm or leg advanced. The arrangement sounds complicated but the effect is exciting and is one which has not been overlooked by the more famous painters of today.

The beginning of the Eighteenth Dynasty saw the emergence of Egypt as a world power, the first of the great empires of the East. Her army contained the dreaded Egyptian bowmen and the new and formidable war chariots, which played such an important part in the famous battle of Kadesh when Ramses II single-handedly defeated the abominable Hittites in his war chariot.

A female Pharaoh now appears upon the scene—Hatshepsut, daughter of Tuthmosis I—and reigned from 1503 to 1482 B.C.

The Nineteenth Dynasty begins with Ramses I who ruled for less than two years. Towards the end of this brief reign Ramses took his son Seti as co-regent.

Seti I was a strong monarch who at once set about retaking for Egypt the provinces she had lost towards the end of the Eighteenth Dynasty. These included Palestine, Tyre, the Phoenician coast and part of Lebanon. Seti I recommenced work on the vast hypostyle hall which his father had started at Karnak. The huge hall was the largest single chamber that the Egyptians ever built, and it was on the north wall of this that Seti's victories were depicted, forming the finest set of battle reliefs in existence.

Seti's tomb in the Valley of the Kings was also on a magnificent scale. It is cut into the living rock to a depth of 300 feet, deeper than the sanctuary of Abu Simbel. Giovanni Belzoni, the Italian explorer of Egyptian antiques, discovered it in 1817. The mummy was missing but the alabaster sarcophagus was intact and now lies in all its beauty in the Sir John Soane Museum, London.

The mummy of Seti I provides an example of the way the priests tried to protect

◀ The temple of Luxor—view towards the colonnade of Amenhotep III showing a seated colossus of Ramses II. The temple was dedicated to Amun in the form of Min and many kings of the XVIIIth and XIXth Dynasties embellished it with the addition of courtyards, colonnades and statues. It was called the "Harem of the South" and once a year the statue of Amun was taken from Karnak on its sacred barque by river to visit his southern residence. The journey was the occasion for a great festival, known as the "Feast of Opet".

Cartouche with the prenomen of Ramses II—"Usermaat-re, Chosen of Re". This name the Greeks interpreted as Osymandias—Shelley's "King of Kings". Modern Greek graffiti are scratched across it.
Temple of Amun. Karnak, Luxor.

the royal dead. The priests, realising it was in danger, removed it in the Twentieth Dynasty to the tomb of Amenophis I. Later it was moved to the tomb of Queen Inhapi, which is the famous mass tomb at Deir-el-Bahri, and, finally, to Cairo in 1881. When the much-travelled mummy was unwrapped in 1886 the embalming had been so well done that Maspero says: "The expression of the face was that of one who had only a few hours previously breathed his last. Death had slightly

Statues of Ramses II represented as Osiris, god of the dead, in the courtyard of the temple of Amun at Luxor. ▶

46

drawn the nostrils and contracted the lips, the pressure of the bandages had flattened the nose a little, and the skin was darkened by the pitch; but a calm and gentle smile still played over the mouth, and the half-opened eyelids allowed a glimpse to be seen from under their lashes of an apparently moist and glistening line—the reflection from the white porcelain eyes let into the orbit at the time of burial."

Ramses II was not the eldest son of his father, Seti I, but he was extremely vain and quickly removed all traces of his elder brother from the record. His first proclamation inscribed at Abydos, a good example of his vanity, reads:

"The Universal Lord himself magnified me whilst I was a child until I became ruler. He gave me the land whilst I was in the egg, the great ones smelling the earth before my face. Then I was inducted as eldest son to be Hereditary Prince upon the throne of Geb (the earth god) and I reported the state of the Two Lands as captain of the infantry and the chariotry. Then when my father appeared in glory before the people, I being a babe in his lap, he said concerning me: 'Crown him as king that I may see his beauty whilst I am alive.' And he called to the chamberlains to fasten the crowns upon my forehead. 'Give him the Great One (the uraeus-serpent) upon his head,' said he concerning me whilst he was on earth." Sir Alan Gardiner, *Egypt of the Pharaohs*, p. 257, Oxford University Press.

In the early years of his reign there was an expedition to Nubia, and it may have been on the return journey that Ramses II gave orders for work to be commenced on the rock temples at Abu Simbel. Meanwhile, in the north the Hittite king, Muwatallish, prepared to resist the power of Egypt. Ramses had also been gathering his forces and in the fifth year of his reign he set out at the head of his army. Muwatallish gathered together surrounding tribes and finally assembled a force of 20,000 troops, including 2,500 chariots holding three men in each, as opposed

◀ Fallen head of Ramses II in the Ramesseum at Thebes.

Highly stylised representations of foreign captives bound with papyrus stems. It may be that the man on the left is a Hittite, the central figure a captive from Esdraelon and the third a north Arabian, but they may simply be conventional figures.   *Temples of Ramses II, Abu Simbel.*

to the forces of Ramses, which consisted of the Egyptian two-man chariots, 8,000 spear men and 9,000 other arms, some 18,000 in all. A most interesting account of this stalemated battle is to be found on the walls of his temple at Abu Simbel.

The treaty with the Hittites ended the warlike ambitions of Ramses and he spent the rest of his long reign of over sixty-six years in erecting monuments to his personal glory. From the Delta to the far south the land was sprinkled with these memorials. He built the city of Pa-Ramessu-mery-Amun. It was here that the

Obelisk of Ramses II outside the first pylon at the temple of Amun at Luxor. The obelisk from the other side of the entrance is now in the Place de la Concorde, Paris. The seated statues are of Ramses II. The grooves in the façade of the pylon were intended to hold the long flagstaffs from which coloured banners fluttered.

Hittite treaty was ratified. In front of the great temple of Tanis Ramses erected the largest statue of himself, 90 feet high. It weighed over 900 tons, but only fragments survive. The Ramesseum at Thebes was built as his own funerary temple and here in the second court he erected another huge statue of himself. This one weighed 1,000 tons but was only 57 feet in height. It too lies in fragments. Obelisks set up in celebration of royal jubilees were numerous and some have travelled far afield. The most famous stands in the Place de la Concorde in Paris. Its twin still stands before the pylon at Luxor. But his most remarkable work and certainly the one for which the world will most remember him is that of the great rock temple of Abu Simbel. Standing in lonely splendour far away from all the hectic activity, politics and intrigue of the courts and cities of the Delta, this grand and solemn monument symbolises the essence of the extraordinary life and religion of those times. In it Ramses II shows himself with the gods and deifies himself to make quite sure that there will be no room for error when he arrives in the Underworld. Every precaution is taken to record his personal deeds of bravery in battle and his worship of the gods. The gods are worshipped with zeal and imagination, until here on earth at Abu Simbel Ramses II is seen to be accepted in their company long before he has passed the Day of Judgment. In the smaller temple his slender daughter-wife, Nefertary, receives similar treatment. He married this beautiful creature before he became a Pharaoh. She bore him two sons to add to the 109 he had by his other wives. He also had 57 daughters, three of whom he married.

Osiride statues of Ramses II in the courtyard of the temple at Luxor. The columns are in the form of stems with capitals shaped like lotus buds. ▶

Overleaf. Osiride figures and a fallen colossus of the king at the Ramesseum on the west bank of the Nile at Thebes. The Ramesseum was the funerary temple of Ramses II where commemorative rites would have been performed for the dead king. Diodorus Siculus called it the "tomb of Osymandias", but the Egyptian name means "House of Millions of Years of Ramses, chosen of Re". It was this statue which inspired Shelley's *Ozymandias* (see page 119).

2: TO SPEAK OF THE DEAD

To speak of the dead is to make them live again—this was one of the beliefs of the Ancient Egyptians.

In the early pre-dynastic period we saw the evidences of expectation of life after death in the furnishing of the primitive graves with the necessities for a future existence, weapons, food, etc. In this age man lived by hunting. The animals and birds which they pursued had qualities which were envied by the hunters, and it was not difficult for them to worship the bird for flight, the wild bull for its strength, the ram for fertility, and so on. This is confirmed by the discovery of cemeteries for bulls, rams, gazelles and even jackals, all carefully wrapped in linen or mats. Cave dwellings of France, Spain and Africa contain even earlier evidence of the relation between man and beast. They are depicted with great beauty in holy places where no doubt the qualities of the animal were transferred to man by sacred rites.

Certain members of the tribe would find themselves elevated to the position of guardians of these sacred places, and with the process of time doubtless discovered

◀ Quarrymen's wedge slots in the granite at Aswan. These quarries provided the granite for most of the building during the time of the Pharaohs. Slots were cut with copper chisels and wooden wedges hammered home and soaked in water. The resulting swelling of the wood split the rock along the line chosen by the mason.
Aswan.

Ramses II holding crook and flail in one hand and *heb-sed* symbol in the other, kneels before Amen-Re, Mut and Khons.

an ability to interpret the needs of the god-beasts and to devise ways of propitiating them with fringe benefits to themselves. The beginning of the complex polytheism of Egyptian religion had already commenced. Each town and district had its favoured animal or bird. The greater the number of gods, the greater the power of the priests. Local gods were popular and had a special place in the affections of the populace of their districts.

With the passage of time man's intelligence increased and he became more than a match for the animals. If the religion was to survive some further step was

Queen Nefertary, wife of Ramses II, standing beside the throne of her husband, holding his leg. She has a headdress sometimes worn by the goddess Hathor—cow's horns either side of a sun's disc and surmounted by feathers. On the side of the throne is the usual representation of two Nile gods binding the *sma*-sign, the hieroglyph for "union". Above it are the names of the king.

Luxor Temple.

The funeral temple of Queen Hatshepsut (1503–1482 B.C.) at Deir-el-Bahri, set in a magnificent natural arena beneath the cliffs on the opposite side of the hill from the Valley of the Kings. Hatshepsut was one of the few women Pharaohs. Her temple is decorated with well-preserved reliefs recording an Egyptian trading expedition to Punt, a country probably situated on the coast of Somalia. *Thebes.*

necessary. Obviously, the gods could not be inferior to man, and it became necessary to elaborate on the original simple formula. The Egyptians had a horror of waste and nothing was ever discarded. The answer lay in compromise—the priests united man and beast. A marriage of human intellect to animal virtues.

The form this usually took was a human figure with the head of an animal or bird. There were exceptions to this, e.g. Hathor—the goddess of love-making, drinking and all the delights of the senses. She had a human body and head but the

The avenue of ram-headed sphinxes at Karnak, attributed to Ramses II.

horns of a cow with the sun's disc between them. She is of special interest to us because the smaller temple at Abu Simbel is in her honour. She was also the goddess of the Western Hills where the area was already sacred to her name five centuries before Ramses II built her temple.

Many of these gods can be seen at Abu Simbel: the falcon-headed Horus, Anubis the jackal-dog, usually found near cemeteries searching for bones, and therefore, with Egyptian practicality, elevated to the position of guardian of the dead. Re-Horakhty of the falcon head is also there—and many others.

Some gods, who may have been introduced at a later period, are entirely human. Osiris is an example of this; indeed, his story bears some resemblance to that of Christ. He became sovereign of Egypt and ruled in a humane manner, teaching men the rudiments of civilisation. He travelled over the world, conquering the minds of men by his wisdom rather than by force. His brother, Set, was jealous of him and conspired to kill him. This he succeeded in doing with the help of confederates and threw the body into the Nile, whence, as the Nile god (one of his many roles), Osiris rises again with each inundation. Isis, his wife, recovered the body and Re, the sun god, sent down his son, Anubis, to wrap the body in bandages like those of a mummy. Isis beat her wings and caused breath to enter it and Osiris moved and lived again. Unable to return to his former life as an earthly king, he reigned in the spirit world and became god of the dead. As god of the dead he did not conflict with any of the living gods, and no Egyptian, whatever his town god, had any difficulty in also adopting Osiris and his creed. This was, essentially, that man lived again in the Underworld after death, provided the proper rites were observed. Every Egyptian finally believed that because Osiris died and rose again to live in eternal blessedness he too could achieve the same destiny provided the requirements of religion had been duly satisfied and that he became one with Osiris. In the great temple at Abu Simbel we can see many huge statues representing Ramses II as Osiris.

Just as Osiris after his death and revival had to be judged, so also would anyone

The colossi of Memnon. These seated statues of Amenophis III once stood before his funerary temple, which has now completely disappeared. They were regarded by the ancients as one of the Wonders of the World. At dawn one of the statues emitted a strange cry, which was thought to be the voice of Memnon (an Ethiopian hero) calling to his mother, Thetis. Pilgrims came to hear this marvel, including the Roman Emperor, Septimius Severus, who decided, as a mark of respect, to rebuild the broken colossus—but Memnon never spoke again.

Luxor, Thebes. XVIIIth Dynasty, c. 1420 B.C.

wishing to share his eternal blessedness. In the great hall of justice the dead person had to appear before forty-two terrible beings. These were the assessors of Osiris, who had now become chief judge. Before each assessor the deceased had to state that he had not committed the sin for which that assessor had authority to punish. This statement is the famous "Negative Confession" which embodies the moral code of the Egyptians. It consists of a series of denials such as: I have not killed; I have not given short measure; I have not spoken falsely; I have not cursed God. No notice, however, is taken of these denials and the deceased is finally led by Horus before his father, Osiris. Here, a balance is set up attended by Anubis, whilst Thoth calculates on his palette the result of weighing the dead man's heart against truth.

Truth is represented by a feather, the symbol of Maet, the goddess of truth, or sometimes by a statuette of the goddess herself wearing an ostrich feather on her head. The two scales of the balance are always shown in equilibrium, which, as the illustrations are all man-made, is presumably the most favourable position for the dead person, the weight of the heart, the instigator of man's actions, being exactly equal to truth. Whether in a sinful person the heart would be heavier or lighter we shall never know unless further excavations bring it to light.

The multiplicity of gods continued. During conflicts and conquests, for various business expediencies, gods of one place became involved with their opposite numbers in another area so that many aspects of the same god can be found today. Except for the Sumerian script the earliest form of writing had been discovered by the Egyptians, which put them ahead of the rest of humanity, but in spite of this they were unable to discard the old ideas when fresh thoughts occurred

The desert road from Wadi Halfa to Abu Simbel (*see page* 93).

Overleaf, left. Nubian girl watering goats in the desert. The water is drawn from a well in a goatskin. The Great Dam will bring untold relief to parched areas such as this.

Overleaf, right. Moslem graves near Abu Simbel. The writing on the tomb in the foreground reads: "In the name of Allah the merciful, there is no god but Allah, and Muhammed is his apostle. This is the grave of the deceased . . ." The rest of the inscription is obscured by the broken dish.

to them. It did not seem inconsistent that diverse theories should hold equal place in their minds.

Egyptian logic also demanded that there must have been a beginning, and their concept of this is markedly similar to the account in the Bible. At first there was nothing but a wilderness of darkness and water. From this emerged the god Atum, who came into existence by himself. He mated with his hand and produced two gods. One of the gods was Shu, who represented the air upon whom all breathing creatures depended and who also held up the sky. The other, the goddess Tfenet, represented the water which surrounded the earth and upon which it floated, easily proved by the fact that if one dug a well one came upon this water. From these two deities all the remainder descended by normal birth.

From this attempt to show something of the confused route taken by Egyptian religion, we come to their even more complex ideas of the manner in which they continued their existence after death. The one thing that is quite clear is that the cheerful, life-loving Egyptians, in common with the rest of humanity, loathed the idea of death and endeavoured to persuade themselves that life continued in another world. Securing this eternal existence required, besides sterling qualities of goodness, some method of obtaining the resurrection of the body and bringing their good deeds forcibly to the attention of the gods. The latter they achieved by the building of temples in which they showed their great achievements and pictured themselves walking with the gods, making gifts to the gods, worshipping the gods, and in the case of Abu Simbel, Ramses II shows himself worshipping his deified self sitting as a god with the other gods. He was not satisfied yet, however. Even in the smaller temple to his wife, Nefertary, he managed to include four huge statues of himself among the six that adorn the outside of the temple, to say nothing of a great many more inside.

◀ Sunrise at Abu Simbel.

Street scene in Wadi Halfa. Soon the town will be inundated by the rising water.

Four Osiride figures of Ramses II in the entrance hall at Abu Simbel.

It was believed that men were created by the gods; the ram god Khnum fashioned them on a potter's wheel; in fact, we see him doing just this in the temple of Luxor. There was, therefore, something divine in man, and he was justified in worshipping the gods and in his turn justified in begging for earthly rewards. The examples of such prayers as have been found show the Egyptians' interest in material things and love of life. The chief demands are for food and drink in plenty, long life, good health and an abundance of material wealth and good living. These are summed up in the prayer of Ramses IV, grandson of the builder of Abu Simbel. He prayed to Osiris as follows:

"And thou shalt give me health, life and old age, a long reign and strength to all my limbs; sight to my eyes, hearing to my ears and pleasure to my heart daily. And thou shalt give me to eat to satiety, and thou shalt give me to drink to drunkenness, and thou shalt promote my seed to be kings in this country to eternity and for ever. And thou shalt make me content every day, thou shalt listen to my voice in whatsoever I shall say to thee and grant me very high Nile floods to furnish thy offerings and to furnish the offerings of the gods and goddesses, the lords of Northern and Southern Egypt, to preserve the sacred bulls, to preserve all the people of thy lands, their cattle and their trees which thy hand has made. For it is thou who hast made them all; thou canst not abandon them to pursue another design with them, for that would not be right."*

Ramses IV also told the god Osiris that he had done more for him in the first four years of his reign than his grandfather had done in sixty-six and therefore Osiris should grant him a longer reign. Osiris, however, was not impressed and the reign of Ramses II's grandson ended two years later.

Occasionally, the Pharaohs made even greater demands on the gods. To become

* Černý, *Ancient Egyptian Religion*, p. 53. Hutchinson.

Panoramic view from the River Nile of the two temples at Abu Simbel. The temple of Ramses II is on the left ▶
and the temple of his Queen, Nefertary, is on the right.

72

a Pharaoh it was essential that one should be the son of a Pharaoh and of a princess of the royal line. To strengthen her feminine position Queen Hatshepsut (1503–1482 B.C.) quickly claimed that she was not the natural daughter of her father, Tuthmosis I, but that her father was the god Amun, the first claim to immaculate conception. Amenophis III, also of doubtful title, followed her example and in Luxor temple, which he gave to the priests in reward for their support for his contention, we see his descent from the god Amun. What the priests accepted, the people did not question.

The priests were intelligent; through the gods they ruled the people and supported the Pharaohs. Their invention of innumerable gods was astounding and their reward was great indeed. The temple at Karnak covered more than 60 acres and could easily accommodate ten European cathedrals. The sun god, Amun, whose house it was, possessed 81,000 slaves, 420,000 head of cattle, 690 acres of land, 83 ships, 46 temples, 65 cities and towns as well as an enormous annual income of gold, silver, copper and precious stones, with food, drink, clothing and everything necessary for the well-being of his devoted servants, in great abundance.

Only on one occasion was the power of the priests challenged and an endeavour made to rationalise the fantastic complexities of the Egyptian polytheism. This happened in the reign of Akhenaten who was married to the beautiful and famous Nefertiti. Akhenaten felt that it was time to rationalise the multiple gods of Egypt and to appoint one supreme being who alone would be worshipped. This he proclaimed was Aten, the sun god, the giver of life, light, warmth and abundance on earth. The priests carried out his wishes but on his death they quickly reverted to the ancient system.

Besides worshipping the gods and building temples in their honour, it was also essential that the physical body be preserved. The ritual for eternal life could only

◀ Head of colossus of Ramses II. The face is thirteen feet from ear to ear and the mouth measures forty-two inches across.   *Façade of the temple of Ramses II, Abu Simbel.*

The Queen-Mother, Mut-Tuy, standing beside the colossal leg of her son, Ramses II. Her hair is dressed in the elaborate plaits, fashionable at the time, and over it she wears the vulture headdress, insignia of queens. Over that she wears another headdress, inscribed with a cartouche and decorated with sacred cobras.

Façade of the temple of Ramses II, Abu Simbel.

succeed if the body was incorruptible. This point of view could be supported in Egypt by the fact that bodies were easily preserved. We have seen that the early inhabitants were preserved by the desiccating quality of the hot, dry desert sand. Had the climate been damp such preservation would not have been possible and no doubt religion would have taken another course. The technique of mummification enabled the royal corpse to rise from the dead to live again, to look after its subjects who, except for the fearless tomb robbers, were dedicated to its preservation.

In its simplest form mummification was the removal of water content of the body by drying, much as strips of meat or fish are dried by primitive peoples even today. In Ptolemaic times a coating of pitch—the Arabic word for pitch is "Mumiya"—was given to the dried cadaver and it was then wrapped in cloth. As some eighty-six per cent of body weight is water, the mummies were comparatively light and subject to attack by insects—hence the protective pitch.

As time went on the processes of mummification became more complex and occasionally defeated their object, as in the case of Tutankhamen whose flesh was unfortunately eaten away by too strong an application of the unguents which were applied to preserve it.

The operation of embalming in its most sophisticated form took a specified period of seventy days to perform and the result was almost permanent. Embalming was a highly-skilled profession, a mixture of surgeon and priest. Arriving at the house of the dead person, the embalmers set up a small tent containing a table upon which the body was laid. First it was washed with water from the Nile. Next, a slit was made in the left side with a flint knife and the organs removed with the exception of the heart, which was required later for the judgment weighing. These were placed in four canopic jars, guarded by their respective goddesses, the wives of the four sons of Horus. Isis guarded the liver, Nephthys the lungs, Neith the stomach and Selket the intestines. These, the most vulnerable, parts were protected in the canopic jars by the addition of natron and aromatic spices and sealed

77

Head of colossus of Ramses II. His cartouche is carved on his shoulder.

Façade of the temple of Ramses II, Abu Simbel.

with ornate lids bearing the likeness of the four sons of Horus and inscribed with texts invoking the help of their wives, the four guardian goddesses.

The body cavity thus emptied was washed out with palm wine and other astringents. The brain was now removed through the nostrils, or, in some cases through an opening made in the ear with an iron instrument. Any residue was dissolved out by the use of cedar oil and other astringents, and the cavity filled with resinous matter. After the foregoing operations the body was packed and covered with natron, a naturally occurring compound of sodium carbonate and sodium bicarbonate, which assisted the process of drying and acted as a preservative just as salt and saltpetre do in the curing of bacon today.

During the seventy days of mummification the priests recited the necessary prayers and incantations which would ensure that the dead man would journey safely to the next world thanks to the example of Osiris. As the ceremony advanced sacred amulets were placed on the body, and finally, when the curing was complete, the bandaging commenced. This started with the extremities. Each finger and toe was separately wrapped and frequently covered with finger and toe stalls of gold or silver. The penis was wrapped in a state of erection. The dried tissues were padded out to their original dimensions with rolls of linen. The body cavities were stuffed with mud, sand and cloth. During the bandaging the correct prayers from the Book of the Dead were intoned and unguents poured on the bandages. More bandages were applied, dipped in myrrh, olive oil, honey, cedar oil, wax and astringents. The correct amount was very important; too much would eat away the flesh and too little would fail to preserve.

After the fingers the forearms were bandaged, then the upper arms, which were folded across the chest and bound in position. In the case of the mummy of Ramses II the left arm has come free from the constriction of the bandages and is raised from the chest as though in a gesture of defiance. Between the layers of bandages were placed all manner of precious things, bracelets, scarabs, pendants, collars—a treasure chest which, alas, far from guaranteeing eternal youth, sexual vigour and a safe passage to the Kingdom of Osiris, generally guaranteed that the royal mummy would be robbed, despoiled and frequently destroyed. Sometimes the priests themselves were in the plot, but generally they did their best to protect the dead Pharaohs, and if they suspected that a royal mummy was in danger they removed it to a safer tomb. The culmination of this saga of the wandering mummies was reached, as we have read, when more than thirty, including Ramses II, were found in a secret cave near the Temple of Queen Hatshepsut at Deir-el-Bahri. They were completely stripped of all wealth but are now safe in the Cairo Museum.

The art of the Egyptian embalmer still causes amazement. Only recently the 1,800-year-old mummy of a girl was discovered in Rome. A bulldozer working near the Via Cassia unearthed a white marble sarcophagus. The English *Sunday Times* of 16th February, 1964, describes the girl: "The body was wrapped in the manner of an Egyptian mummy; a number of the girl's playthings: a doll, a cup, a shell and an amphora were beside her."

When the wrapping was taken off the body there was a strong smell of eucalyptus from the embalming fluid. The girl's skin, at first pale, became bronzed when it was brought into contact with the air. Her auburn hair had been long and was covered with pitch to preserve it. Her features were still delicate and beautiful. She wore gold ear-rings in pierced ears and a blue stone necklace. On the little finger of her left hand a gold ring carried a winged-victory emblem. The Italian Egyptologists who examined the body claim that the embalming was done in Egypt. It was so perfect that they were able to take her finger-prints. Such skill in embalming was unknown in Roman times. Indeed such skill is still unknown today. The most advanced method used by morticians of the West consists of exchanging part of the body fluids for a weak solution of formaldehyde and injecting the viscera with the same liquid until a proper degree of sterility is reached. Such embalming is of a temporary nature, rarely lasting for more than a few weeks. Like the Egyptians, the operator uses cosmetics and padding to produce a lifelike effect.

Three-quarter view of the head of a colossus of Ramses II. The king's title: "King of Upper and Lower Egypt" and his cartouche are written above his head. The ears are marked with a depression showing that they were pierced for earrings. *Façade of the temple of Ramses II, Abu Simbel.*

The mummy is now completely wrapped, the amulets are all in place and the priest pronounces the final benediction: "You live again, you live again forever, here you are young once more forever." The mummy is then placed in a sheath of wood or metal. In the case of Tutankhamen this was made of pure gold and weighed 2,600 pounds and was worked to resemble his features. This sheath, in turn, is placed inside another and perhaps one more until it is finally placed inside the huge stone sarcophagus in the burial chamber of the tomb.

The mind reels at the treasure which must have accompanied the great Ramses, aged nearly one hundred years, after sixty-six years of a glorious reign. Alas, according to a papyrus in the British Museum, his tomb was pillaged by his own priests.

The dwelling place and occupation of the blessed dead are subject to an extraordinary confusion of ideas. Broadly speaking, the Egyptians pictured life after death as being similar to life on earth, with similar requirements. Thus their tombs contained all the necessities for normal living, especially food and drink. At first these were actually real and were sent by the relatives to the tomb guardian, but later they were simply pictures on the walls of the tomb.

Occasionally scepticism regarding the future of life was expressed. One such example is the Song of the Harper inscribed on the wall of a tomb. It is below the figure of a harpist and advises a hedonistic approach to life. T. E. Peet. *The Literatures of Egypt, Palestine and Mesopotamia*, p. 59.

"Rejoice and let thy heart forget that day when they shall lay thee to rest.

"Cast all sorrow behind thee, and bethink thee of joy until there come that day of reaching port in the land that loveth silence.

Façade of the temple of Ramses II. Two seated colossi of the king, sixty-five feet high, flank the doorway, ▶ above which stands Re-Horakhty, as its guardian. Between the colossi are standing statues of Queen Nefertary, princes and princesses. The head of the second figure from the left lies broken below the platform.

Abu Simbel.

The headless statue at Abu Simbel. The missing head lies, shattered by an earthquake, in the forecourt below.

"Follow thy desire as long as thou livest, put myrrh on thy head, clothe thee in fine linen.

"Set singing and music before thy face.

"Increase yet more the delights which thou hast, and let not thy heart grow

Head and shoulders of colossus of Ramses II. *Façade of the temple of Ramses II, Abu Simbel.*

faint. Follow thine inclination and thy profit (?). Do thy desires upon earth, and trouble not thine heart until that day of lamentation come to thee.

"Spend a happy day and weary not thereof. Lo, none may take his goods with him, and none that hath gone may come again."

We have seen that the simplest form of burial was to place the body in the sand. The form of Moslem burial today is, in a modest way, like that of Ancient Egypt. A grave is dug some six feet deep and a chamber excavated on one side which receives the cloth-wrapped body. The side containing the body is then bricked up and the grave filled in. The tombs of the Pharaohs were very much more elaborate but worked on the same principle. A vertical or sloping shaft was driven into the rock from which several chambers were excavated. These were for the mummy, the statue of the Ka, household goods and treasure, food and the necessities of life. With the mummy was the Book of the Dead to help the deceased on his passage through the underworld, and *Ushabti*-figures. The Pharaohs, being kings and gods, did not have to labour in the life hereafter, but the ordinary person considered that just as he had to work on earth, so there would be ploughing, planting and irrigating in the next world, and that no one would be exempt from this work. True, the fields would be eternally fruitful and the corn would be seven cubits high with ears two cubits long, but someone would have to do the work. This would be acceptable to a manual labourer, but for the scribes and nobles the idea of such work spoiled completely their conception of paradise. However, the fertile imagination of the Egyptians soon solved the matter by the introduction of a small Osiride statuette called a *Ushabti*-figure or "answerer" who would be magically animated in the hereafter, and when his master was called upon to do some work the *Ushabti*-figure would answer the roll-call and work in his place.

Head of Queen Nefertary, wife of Ramses II. Over her vulture headdress she wears a crown composed of ▶ sacred cobras with a cartouche in the centre. The statue stands beside the seated colossi of Ramses II.
Façade of the temple of Ramses II, Abu Simbel.

Chapter 6 of the Book of the Dead reads, "O thou, this Ushabti, if thou art commanded to do what is to be done in the nether world of various kinds of work, then say, Here I am." This insurance against hard work was carried to great lengths, and as time went on the number of *Ushabti*-figures grew until there was one for each day of the year. Later still there were as many as 700 so that they had to be divided into groups carrying the requisite implements for their labour and controlled by *Ushabti*-figures of foremen carrying whips. To avoid the possibility of quarrelling there were enough *Ushabtis* for each day of the year, and written on the wall of the tomb was the warning, "Obey only him who made thee"—an admonition which was clearly to prevent them from going off and working for someone else.

Originally the mortuary temple and tomb of a Pharaoh stood side by side, but as the danger of tomb-robbing became acute the tombs were moved farther and farther away from the temples to remote and inaccessible spots, where their entrances were covered with the natural surface debris, so that it should have been impossible to locate them. Inevitably, however, the priests and builders knew where they were and the lure of treasure undid the best-laid schemes. The tombs have been despoiled by robbers, and so, alas, have the temples, due to the tireless efforts of the Copts, who regarded the serene statues as pagan affronts to Christianity. How they must have toiled over the centuries, chipping off ears and noses, levering statues off their thrones. The havoc is truly frightful. Fortunately, Abu Simbel was covered with sand and so escaped most of their self-righteous wrath. In spite of the destruction, Egypt still possesses enough remains to fill the viewer with wonder that so much beauty could have been wrought from the hard rock with such primitive tools.

The temples were built in praise of the gods and to establish the records of the Pharaohs, showing their deeds on wall inscriptions, rather like magnificent strip cartoons. The famous Battle of Kadesh is so depicted, with the victorious Ramses smiting his foes single-handed and scattering them in all directions on the walls of the great rock temple at Abu Simbel.

3: THE WAY TO ABU SIMBEL

The way to Abu Simbel lies across the desert or upon the waters of the Nile. The road across the desert starts from Wadi Halfa. The easiest approach is by air from Khartoum. Wadi Halfa itself is a flourishing, well-irrigated town, stretching down to the Nile and lying only a few feet above the river. Like the rest of the area, it will be flooded when the High Dam comes into operation.

At Wadi Halfa it is possible to hire a motor-car to do the trip to Abu Simbel. In order to reach the temples before sun-up one leaves Wadi Halfa, which is on the east bank of the Nile, at three o'clock in the morning. At first the way lies through little villages set in their strips of irrigation. The mud walls are gaily painted and the houses picturesquely set around ancient trees and landmarks. Here, as in the rest of the Nile Valley, there is a sharp division between the desert and cultivation. On one side of the road women are harvesting the ripe gold corn, whilst a few feet away a Moslem cemetery marks the beginning of the limitless desert. Each grave has a broken shard or some household vessel beside the headstone—a link with customs of the ancient past.

Finally, the strips of irrigation vanish and there is open desert. The potholes of

◀ Head and shoulders of a colossus of Ramses II. *Abu Simbel.*

Ramses II looking out over the Nile. Beside the king are statues of the princesses Nebttaui, Bentanat and another not named. Near these statues is an inscription which records the marriage of Ramses II with a Hittite princess, who was given the Egyptian name, Matneferure. Her father, Khetsasar, is shown presenting her to Ramses II. The battle of Kadesh took place in the fifth year of Ramses's reign. The marriage was celebrated in the thirty-fourth year of his reign, after several more campaigns in Syria. *Façade of the temple of Ramses II, Abu Simbel.*

civilisation disappear and a dozen alternative sandy trails spread out. Motoring in the desert has to be fast—fifty to sixty miles per hour—to prevent bogging down in patches of soft sand. Here and there steep hills of reddish-black rock jut out of the

Nile gods of Upper and Lower Egypt binding the flowers symbolic of the two parts of the country, the lily and the papyrus, to the hieroglyphic sign for "union". Above is the cartouche of Ramses II. ▶
Façade of the temple of Ramses II, Abu Simbel.

94

undulating desert and occasionally the road weaves in and out of drifts of black crystalline stones about the size of oranges.

Should a car bog down in soft sand, as it often does, the driver and his assistant get out wire mesh and thick mats, relics of the desert campaign. The sand is dug away and the mats placed on top of the mesh to give the wheels purchase. Everyone pushes and soon firmer ground is reached.

In the distance a range of sandstone hills marks the proximity of the Nile. Half an hour later a strip of green appears: it is the beginning of the green-lined irrigation channels of the orderly village opposite Abu Simbel. One tends to think of the rock temples as being buried far from the haunts of man. In fact, the village itself is just one half a mile away on the opposite side of the Nile. Its irrigated land must extend over several hundreds of acres.

To reach the temples it is necessary to cross the Nile in one of the feluccas which patiently wait for custom.

The Nile boat has not changed much since the time of Ramses himself. The boatman tacks his craft across the milky green water and with the first pale light in the sky the temples become visible. They seem at this distance much less imposing. Cut into the long sandstone cliffs which rise high above them, the colossi are overshadowed, but as the felucca gets nearer the perspective improves in their favour, and as the boat lands the effect is magnificent.

After grounding on the narrow strip of bright yellow sand which fronts the temple the boatman runs out a single springy plank for his passengers. If the trip has been correctly timed, the sun should be nearing the horizon. Inside, in the interior of the great temple, the eight huge Osiride statues of Ramses II wait for

Colossal figure of the god Re-Horakhty, falcon-headed and wearing the sun's disc and sacred uraeus-cobra. The figure, which stands above the doorway of the temple of Ramses II, holds in his hands the sign of "life" and is flanked by the emblems of the goddess Maet (Truth) and Anubis (god of embalmment).

Façade of the temple of Ramses II, Abu Simbel.

Overleaf. Falcons, sacred to the god Horus, standing at the feet of the seated colossus of Ramses II. Queen Nefertary stands beside her husband.

Temple of Ramses II, Abu Simbel.

The Viceroy of Nubia, Yuny, holding a fan, greets Ramses II. Unfinished rock-carving near the temple of Queen Nefertary. *Abu Simbel.*

the first light. Beyond them lies the second chamber and beyond that the small antechamber leading to the sanctuary, cut 180 feet into the living rock. Suddenly, the sun rises and gradually the cold darkness is suffused with its warm golden light. It is only on two days of each year that the sun actually shines directly on the four gods in the innermost sanctuary, the 23rd of February and the 23rd of October. The effect, nevertheless, is always remarkable. The reflected light

◀ Four figures of Ramses II inside his temple at Abu Simbel. The king is represented as Osiris, god of the dead. On the ceiling are painted vultures with outstretched wings, sacred to Nekhbet, goddess of el-Kab.

transforms every corner, and the pale colours that the painters used more than 3,200 years ago can be seen. In the sanctuary the four gods—Ptah, Amen-Re, Ramses and Re-Horakhty—sit in equal dignity on one massive throne. Standing in the centre of the floor before them is a cube of rock, the support for the sacred boat which was for the use of the dead Pharaoh. Made of wood and not dissimilar in construction to the felucca, these sacred boats have not been able to withstand the passage of time.

Beside the seated figures of the gods the walls of the sanctuary teem with life. The work is carried out in low relief sculpture, still bearing a remarkable amount of the original stone ground colours, blue, orange, red and green, while the many varieties of shade show up delicately in the reflected light, which carves dark shadows in the deeply etched reliefs. The work becomes progressively stronger as one leaves the innermost chambers, as if the artists did not wish to stay near the gods—or perhaps the atmosphere may have been too suffocating to permit proper concentration on the work.

The general layout of the temple is impressive—the immense proportions of the Osiride pillars, the high square-cut walls, and the ceilings still maintained by the solid rock as the ancient masons designed them. A closer look shows that every inch of the rock surface is carved and that most of the carvings are coloured. It is a giant tapestry in stone, not only of life in the next world but also of the exploits of Ramses himself. Moving from the sanctuary outwards, through the small ante-chamber, the worn sandstone floor leads to the smaller of the halls, 36 feet broad by 25 feet deep. The ceiling is supported by four square pillars carved with sculptures of Ramses with the gods. He is making offerings to Isis, Min-Amun and himself; he is a living god king but he has also established himself as a god in

Osiride statue of Ramses II startlingly emerges from the dark background as the rising sun enters the temple. ▶
He wears a linen kilt covered by an apron from which hang gold images of the sacred cobra. The buckle of
his belt is inscribed with his cartouche.   *Temple of Ramses II, Abu Simbel.*

the kingdom of the dead and is content that his living self should worship his deified self. On the south side of the entrance he similarly worships himself, Amen-Re and Mut. On the north wall he makes offerings to the sacred boat carried on the shoulders of the priests and is accompanied by his queen, Nefertary; this is repeated on the south wall. On the rear wall he worships Re-Horakhty and Amen-Re.

As the sun rises, the light moves slowly across the sandy floor leading one to the great entrance hall, 54 feet broad and 58 feet deep. The eight huge Osiride figures of Ramses, sharply picked out against the light, make an even more impressive sight seen from here than from the entrance. The figures on the south side wear the White Crown of Upper Egypt, those on the north the Double Crown of Upper and Lower Egypt. The figures are well preserved, and as they stretch some thirty feet from floor to ceiling their presence is overpowering. The remaining sides of the column from which they spring are covered with scenes of Ramses before the various gods: Horus, Atum, Thoth, Min, Khnum, Amen-Re, Ptah, Re-Horakhty, Hathor, Isis and two goddesses of the Nile, Satet and Anukis. He is making offerings, dancing or holding hands and generally creating the impression that he is a welcome friend.

To some extent the work so far is stylised and repetitious, as indeed is most of the work of the Ancient Egyptians . . . the left foot in advance of the right, the head in profile, the expression serene. This is not so with the procession of events that is depicted on the walls of the next chamber. This is a great historical pageant, like an oriental Bayeux Tapestry. Immediately to the right of the entrance is an excellent relief of Ramses, always twice the size of his enemies, pounding a group of Asiatic prisoners on the head with the hilt of his mace. The Asiatics are holding up their hands in pitiful submission as they kneel in a composite group, like a many-armed and headed idol. Above Ramses flies the vulture Nekhbet, and

Osiride figures standing before square pillars which are decorated with representations of the king making offerings to various deities. *Temple of Ramses, Abu Simbel.* ▶

behind him is the symbol of his Ka. Below the ground level on which he stands is a row of his numerous daughters playing sistra, musical instruments consisting of an oval frame carrying pieces of metal which rattle when shaken. (Cleopatra made use of a large number of sistra at the Battle of Actium in 31 B.C.) Tucked away in a corner is the name of the sculptor, Piyay, son of Khanufer.

Continuing along the right-hand wall is the famous march of the Egyptian army under Ramses to Kadesh. It was this drawn battle that provided Ramses with a reputation on which he was able to live for the remainder of his very long life. In the spring of the fifth year of his reign Ramses led his army of about 18,000 against Egypt's old enemies, the Hittites. After four weeks' marching he found himself on the heights overlooking the fortified town of Kadesh, now Tel Neby Mend. The town lay on the banks of the Orontes, now the River Asi, north of Beirut and some four hundred miles from the Egyptian frontier. It held a key position guarding the main route that any north- or south-bound army had to take.

The army of Ramses was divided into four divisions, Amun who led the van, followed by the divisions of Re, Ptah and Sutekh. As Ramses waited for his long-drawn-out columns to catch up with him, two prisoners were brought in who declared that Muwatallish, the Hittite king, had retreated to Aleppo in fear of the advance of the Egyptian forces. Delighted with this news, Ramses immediately pressed on and camped before the town of Kadesh without waiting for the rest of his army. He sent messengers to tell his division of Amun to cut off any retreat to the north-west and to prevent any assistance coming from that direction. Whilst Ramses was enjoying his meal in anticipation of a triumphal entry into Kadesh two Hittite spies were captured who, after a severe beating, which is faithfully portrayed on the wall, confessed:

◀ Seated figures of the deified Ramses II and Re-Horakhty. The king was represented the same size as the god, whom he regarded not only as protector but as partner. *Sanctuary of the temple of Ramses II, Abu Simbel.*

Left: Ramses II anoints Min-Amun-Kamutef, a composite deity comprising Min of Coptos, an ancient fertility god, Amun of Thebes, Chief of the pantheon during the New Kingdom and Kamutef, a Theban ithyphallic deity —"The Bull of his Mother". *Right:* Seated statues of Ptah, god of Memphis, who created the world by means of utterance, and Amen-Re king of the gods. *Temple of Ramses II, Abu Simbel.*

The battle of Kadesh on the river Orontes in Syria where Ramses II so nearly met a disastrous end. On the left are the Egyptian chariots still in good order; facing them the enemy's horses, pierced by Egyptian arrows, stumble and fall, throwing the warriors to the ground. *Temple of Ramses II, Abu Simbel.*

Ramses II trampling on one Libyan and slaying another.

" 'See, the wretched Chief of Khatti is come together with the many foreign countries who are with him, whom he has brought with him as allies, the land of Dardany, the land of Nahrin, that of Keshkesh, those of Masa, those of Pidasa, the land of Karkisha and Luka, the land of Carahemish, the land of Arzawa, the land of Ugarit, that of Arwen (?), the land of Inesa, Mushanet, Kadesh, Khaleb, and the entire land of Kedy. They are furnished with their infantry and their chariotry carrying their weapons of warfare, and they are more numerous than the sands of the river-banks. See, they stand equipped and ready to fight behind Kadesh the old'." Sir Alan Gardiner, *The Kadesh Inscriptions of Rameses II*, p. 29. Griffith Institute, Oxford.

Ramses II, wearing the Blue Crown, leads Nubian captives, tied together in fantastic poses, to Amen-re, the deified Ramses II and Mut. *Temple of Ramses II, Abu Simbel.*

The anger of Ramses on learning this news was instant and terrible. He was alone with a handful of household troops whilst his four divisions were straggling out behind him, easy victims for the wily Muwatallish.

It did not take the Hittites long to strike. They poured down on the unprepared division of Re, who fled in utter confusion to the division of Amun. The forces of Amun were, however, in no better position to withstand the onslaught than the division of Re, and, further hindered by the panic of the fugitives, they too were swept away in a disastrous rout. The remaining two divisions, unaware of the fate of their brethren, were still proceeding slowly in the direction of Kadesh. At this moment, by all the laws of battle, Ramses was a beaten man. In fact, this was his hour of greatness. He had no shortage of personal valour and flair. Calling for his chariot and horses and for Menna, his shield-bearer, he flung himself into a series of headlong charges which held the Hittite forces until his remaining divisions appeared upon the scene and drove them from the field.

These scenes are depicted with great verve and the writer relates them, no doubt with Ramses' point of view firmly in mind, in the flowery language of the period. The translation is from *Egypt of the Pharaohs* by Sir Alan Gardiner, p. 262.

"Then His Majesty arose like his father Mont and took the accoutrements of battle, and girt himself with his corselet; he was like Baal in his hour, and the great pair of horses which bore His Majesty, belonging to the great stable of Usimareset-penre, beloved of Amun, were named Victory-in-Thebes. Then His Majesty started forth at a gallop, and entered into the host of the fallen ones of Khatti, being alone by himself, none other with him. And His Majesty went to look about him, and found surrounding him on his outer side 2,500 pairs of horses with all the champions of the fallen ones of Khatti and of the many countries who were with them, from Arzawa, Masa, Pidasa, Keshkesh, Arwen, Kizzuwadna, Khaleb, Ugarit, Kadesh, and Luka; they were three men to a pair of horses as a unit, whereas there was no captain with me, no charioteer, no soldier of the army, no shield-bearer; my infantry and chariotry melted away before them, not one of them stood firm to fight with them. Then said His Majesty: What ails thee, my father Amun? Is it a father's part to ignore his son? Have I done anything without thee, do I not walk and halt at thy bidding? I have not disobeyed any course commanded by thee. How great is the great lord of Egypt to allow foreigners to draw nigh in his path! What careth thy heart, O Amun, for these Asiatics so vile and ignorant of God? Have I not made for thee very many monuments and filled thy temple with my booty, and built for thee my Mansion of Millions of Years and given thee all my wealth as a permanent possession and presented to thee all lands together to enrich thy offerings, and have caused to be sacrificed to thee tens of thousands of cattle and all

Horses drawing the chariot in which the king returns from war in Nubia with his captives. A bowman walks ahead and the king's pet lion runs beside the horses. *Temple of Ramses II, Abu Simbel.*

manner of sweet-scented herbs? No good deeds have I left undone . . . What will men say if even a little thing befall him who bends himself to thy counsel?"

Fortified by his prayers to Amun, Ramses rallied his shield-bearer, Menna, who not unnaturally was intimidated by the odds of 2,500 to 1. The poem continues with Menna saying:

The king offers lettuces to Min-Amun and Isis. Lettuces were regarded as an aphrodisiac. *Second Hall, Temple of Ramses II, Abu Simbel.* ▶

" ' My good Lord, thou strong Ruler, thou great saviour of Egypt on the day of fighting, we stand alone in the midst of the battle. Behold, the infantry and chariotry have deserted us, for what reason dost thou remain to rescue them? Let us get clear and do thou save us, O Usimaresetpenre.' Then said His Majesty to his shield-bearer: 'Stand firm, steady thy heart, my shield-bearer. I will enter in among them like the pounce of a falcon, killing, slaughtering, and casting to the ground. What careth thy heart for these effeminate ones at millions of whom I take no pleasure?' Thereupon His Majesty started forth quickly and entered at a gallop into the midst of the battle for the sixth time of entering in amongst them."*

There can be little doubt that Ramses' bold attack saved the day. The advancing Hittite chariots had pursued the divisions of Re and Amen to exhaustion and were unprepared for any resistance. Ramses obviously also had the assistance of his household troops, and under his leadership a series of headlong charges drove the spent forces of the Hittites back to the river bank. Muwatallish, watching the battle from the eastern bank of the Orontes, inexplicably failed to throw in 8,000 spearmen which he had held all along in reserve. Meanwhile, the divisions of Ptah and Setekh, as already related, had driven the Hittites off the field into Kadesh.

The next day the severed hands of the slain were presented to Ramses, and his troops were loud in their praises of their leader. Ramses, however, reminded them that he had had to deal with the enemy single-handed and reserved his praises for his shield-bearer, Menna, and for his two horses, "Victory in Thebes" and "Mut is Satisfied", who had so successfully drawn his chariot. He gave orders that they should be fed in his presence when he was in his palace.

Summing up, the Battle of Kadesh could easily have been won by the Hittites if they had used all their forces, but for some reason their strong brigade of infantry

* Taken from Sir Alan Gardiner, *The Kadesh Inscriptions of Rameses II*, Oxford.

Amen-Re, king of the gods, seated upon a throne, presents the symbol of life to the king's nostrils.
Temple of Ramses II, Abu Simbel.

King offering wine to a human-headed god. *Temple of Ramses II, Abu Simbel.*

was never used at all. Had they been brought in at the right moment, Ramses' valiant charge would have been useless and the Egyptian forces annihilated. As it turned out, neither side won. Ramses did not proceed to take Kadesh but returned home as rapidly as possible to relate the story of his great victory, which, in fact, was nothing more than the story of his personal valour overcoming his bad generalship. The poem written about the battle and scenes from it were repeated throughout Egypt whenever the opportunity occurred. Besides Abu Simbel, the tale is told on papyri and at Karnak, Luxor, Abydos and the Ramesseum, which also contains the largest and heaviest statue of Ramses, weighing over one thousand tons. It is of this statue, now sadly fallen and defaced, that Shelley wrote his poem *Ozymandias*.

I met a traveller from an antique land
Who said: "Two vast and trunkless legs of stone
Stand in the desert . . . Near them, on the sand,
Half sunk, a shattered visage lies, whose frown,
And wrinkled lip and sneer of cold command,
Tell that its sculptor well those passions read
Which yet survive, stamped on these lifeless things,
The hand that mocked them, and the heart that fed.
And on the pedestal these words appear:
'My name is Ozymandias, king of kings:
Look on my works, ye Mighty, and despair!'
Nothing beside remains. Round the decay
Of that colossal wreck, boundless and bare,
The lone and level sands stretch far away."

The poem might equally well have been written of the second colossus at Abu Simbel whose head lies shattered at its feet, though it is hard to imagine the serene sculptured face of Ramses wearing either a frown or a wrinkled lip. As for the sneer

All that remains of the tomb of Ramses the Great.

Detail of illustration on page 114. The horse has a bronze bit in its mouth. ▶
Temple of Ramses II, Abu Simbel.

Overleaf, left. Ramses II tramping on one Libyan and smiting another. Ramses probably fought against the Libyans during the early years of his reign. Libyans and other tribes dwelling in the western deserts made incursions from time to time into the fertile and attractive land of the Delta. They were a fair-skinned people, partly nomadic. By the latter part of Ramses's reign many of them had become soldiers in his army.
Great Hall of the Temple of Ramses II, Abu Simbel.

Overleaf, right. Ramses II offering papyrus flowers and Nefertary offering a sistrum and a papyrus flower to the goddess Hathor.
Vestibule of the Queen's Temple, Abu Simbel.

of cold command, it does not exist, the numerous faces of Ramses have all the same tranquil expression (similar to that usually associated with the Buddha).

The name Ozymandias appears to be a corruption of User-Maet-Re, the prenomen of Ramses which is used at Abu Simbel.

The sequel to the Battle of Kadesh came on the 28th of November in the twenty-first year of Ramses, when envoys arrived from the Hittite court with the final terms of a treaty between the two monarchs. This agreed, amongst other things, that neither party would invade the territory of the other and that they would assist each other if attacked by an outside power. It is the first known instance of an international agreement, and considering that it was made over three thousand years ago it is very modern in its terms. The treaty was faithfully kept, and in the thirty-fourth year of his reign was further strengthened by the marriage of Ramses to a Hittite princess. This scene is also inscribed on the walls of Abu Simbel.

As the sun rises it retreats from the sanctuary until it spills a bright pool of light in the great doorway. It was here in 1871 that the circus strong man and splendid explorer Belzoni, after clearing away the sand, became the first European to enter the temple. The temple itself had been discovered by Burckhardt in 1812, but at that time the river of fine sand that flows down between the two temples had covered the larger one so that the head of only one colossus appeared above the drift. It was this constant cataract of dry sand that protected the temple from erosion and from the fanatical fury of the Copts.

The sand was cleared on numerous occasions but always returned. James Baikie, the Scottish theologian, writes: "It is to be feared that man will, here as elsewhere, wage a fruitless battle in the end against nature, and that the great temple will finally be buried." He continues prophetically that "completion of its destiny will not come, however, until man has ceased to value one of the greatest works

Ramses II offers the image of Maet, goddess of Truth, to Thoth, the ibis-headed god of Wisdom who is wearing on his head the moon's disc and horns. In front of the throne are offering stands decorated with papyrus flowers.
Temple of Ramses II, Abu Simbel.

Hathor being offered flowers by Ramses, and sistra and flowers by Nefertary. *Abu Simbel.*

of the past sufficiently to consider it worth protection". Today Egyptians are still loading the sand on to miniature trucks and tipping it into the placid Nile.

Even with the protective coat of sand, time has not been kind to the statues of

126

the great temple. As early as fifty years after its completion, Seti II had to patch up the third colossus from the south. Nature had already begun her attack on the arrogance of man. Years later the head of the second colossus fell to the ground. The leg of this colossus bears a Greek inscription to the effect that the army of King Psammetichus, son of Theocles, passed this way and went on by Cercis as far as the river permitted. This was written in the Twenty-sixth Dynasty, 593–588 B.C. Since then, many lesser mortals have added their names to the statues, thus demonstrating that the desire for immortality is not confined to the mighty—but is universal.

The forecourt in front of the colossi is empty and nowhere is there evidence of the houses where the priests who attended the temple would have lived. There must

Priests carrying the barque of the deified Ramses II. *Second Hall, temple of Ramses II, Queen's Temple, Abu Simbel.*

have been a considerable number of servants, for the gods had a daily service of washing, clothing and feeding just as any living person would require. The order of daily temple ritual is preserved for us on the walls of the temple of Osiris at Abydos, and similar ceremonies would have taken place at Abu Simbel. Professor Cerný gives an excellent account of the liturgy in his book *Ancient Egyptian Religion*:

"Before entering the temple the priest had to purify himself in the sacred pool. On his arrival at the temple he first kindled a fire and filled a censer with burning charcoal and incense. He then proceeded towards the shrine in which the god had spent the night. He broke the clay seal on the door, pushed away the bolts and opened the two wings. The statue of the god appeared to him and the priest saluted the god, casting himself upon the ground before the statue. He then chanted one or more hymns and offered honey to the god, burning more incense while making four circumambulations around the statue. Sometimes he offered the deity a figure of Maet, the goddess of Truth. Finally, he took the statue out of its shrine, removed the old clothing and anointed it with unguent."

After this the toilet of the god or gods takes place.

"The priest again censed the deity and sprinkled it with water out of four namset-vessels and four red vessels. After repeating the censing he cleaned the statue's mouth with three different kinds of natron and dressed it with the head-cloth and garments of various colours, replacing its jewels, anointed it and painted its eyelids with green and black eye paints. Finally, he invested the god with the royal insignia."

Next followed the repast.

"The priest purified the altar and then laid food and drink before the god. He raised each course separately, offering it to the god. The banquet finished, he closed the door of the shrine and sealed it. He purified the room, removing his footsteps

Ramses II smiting Libyan prisoners. On pillars are figures of Thoth, ibis-headed; Anukis, wearing a tall head- ▶
dress; and Horus, falcon-headed. *Great Hall, temple of Ramses II, Abu Simbel.*

with special care and left the room. At every stage in the ceremony the priest recited appropriate words or formulae."

From the forecourt an inclined plane leads to a low terrace on which stand the thrones of the colossi. Their footstools are some eight feet high and on either side of the entrance are rows of captives, arms pinioned behind their backs and neck tied to neck. Those on the north side are Asians whilst those on the south side are Negroes. Above the captives are representations of the Nile gods binding together papyrus and lotus, the emblems of Lower and Upper Egypt, in a symbol of unity.

Along coping stones which line the narrow terrace stands a row of hawks and statues of the king; these statues are only a few feet high and serve to emphasise the dignity and size of the colossi.

The total width of the temple is 119 feet and the height is over 100 feet. The colossi are 65 feet high, 25 feet across the shoulders. The ears are $3\frac{1}{2}$ feet in length. More important than mere size is the effect of gentle serenity and warmth which they seem to exude. There is an atmosphere of endless patience as they calmly await the dawn. As the sun rises the moving shadows slowly alter their expressions, until it sinks once more and leaves them in the darkness of their underworld. High above the statues on the cornice which frames the group sits a row of dog-headed apes, sacred to the rising sun; they watch for the dawn and from their lofty vantage point are the first to see the early light and to reassure the Pharaoh.

Round the feet of the statues members of the royal family peep out between the giant legs. On the first colossus are Princess Nebbtaui, Princess Bentanat and an unidentified princess. On the second and headless colossus are the king's mother,

Osiride figure of the king from the interior of the temple of Ramses II. By the side of his head is inscribed the beginning of the royal titles: "The good god, Lord of the Two Lands . . ." followed by his cartouches: "Ramses, beloved of Amun". The king is here represented as Osiris, god of the Dead, who wears the White Crown of Upper Egypt and carries a crook and flail, symbols of his powers. *Temple of Ramses II, Abu Simbel.*

Ramses II smiting his Libyan captives. He wears the Double Crown and brandishes a mace—he also wears the ritualistic tail which was a very ancient part of the royal apparel. Behind the king is a standard inscribed with his Horus-name: "Mighty Bull, beloved of Maet". The standard itself holds an emblem: the head of the king surmounted by the signs meaning "double of the king". It is not known exactly when or where this battle took place. Possibly it was early in the reign. However, highly stylised scenes of this type are frequently carved on temple walls and do not always mean that an actual battle took place. Just visible below the feet of the king are the heads of some of his daughters holding sistra—bronze rattles decorated with the face of the goddess Hathor.   *Temple of Ramses II, Abu Simbel.*

Queen Mut-Tuy, Queen Nefertary and one of Ramses' "hundred and eleven" sons, Prince Amen(hir)khopshef. On the third, Queen Nefertary appears twice and Prince Ramses. On the fourth, Nefertary appears once again, and between the huge legs is a defaced child. It is quite clear that his daughter Nefertary, whom he

Ramses II followed by his *ka*, or *double*, smites Nubian prisoners whom he is holding by their hair, in the presence of Amen-Re, king of the gods.   *Temple of Ramses II, Abu Simbel.*

married before he became a Pharaoh, was also very much his favourite wife. No other wives appear, but Nefertary is kept in her place, which is about halfway up to the Pharaoh's knee. For all that, she is entirely captivating in her diaphanous gown with her breasts just showing below her shoulder-length hair.

On the rock wall at the left-hand side of the terrace Ramses is seated between two gods, with the king of the Hittites and his daughter worshipping him. In a recess set above the entrance, in the place of honour, is the figure of Re-Horakhty, falcon-headed and crowned with the solar disc. On his left is the jackal-headed staff,

User, and on his right the figure of Maet, the whole group thus making the prenomen User-Maet-Re of Ramses. On either side Ramses makes offerings to the central figure, once more taking for granted his credit in the Underworld.

Just north of the fourth colossus lies an open chapel dedicated to the sun-god. It was discovered by M. Barsanti in 1910 and is partly rock-hewn and partly built of stone. The entrance is from the terrace, and, as in the main temple, the walls are covered with scenes of Ramses with the gods. They are badly mutilated, but four praying figures who originally stood upon the altar have been removed, with other small obelisks and figures, to the safety of Cairo Museum.

Holding a similar position, but to the south, is another small chapel discovered in 1874 by Miss Amelia Edwards. This, too, is partly rock-hewn and partly built. It shows Ramses with his Ka offering to the boat of Re-Horakhty and to the boat of Thoth.

Sheltering between the side of the cliff and the first colossus is an alien tomb of plain, polished granite which contains the body of Major Tidswell, who died during the Nile Expedition of 1884.

The smaller or queen's temple lies about 150 yards north of the main temple and faces south-east rather than almost due east, as is the case with the larger temple. It looks small by comparison but its measurements are still impressive. The width is 92 feet and the height 39 feet. The method of design differs in that the figures are all standing. In between each of them are solid buttresses bearing inscriptions. In all there are six figures: four of Ramses and two of his wife. Nefertary appears between the statues of Ramses. As already described, she wears a transparent gown, with her hair framing her face and flowing over her shoulders. On her head she wears the solar disc and the ostrich feathers of royalty.

Once more round the huge legs tiny, knee-high children peep. The queen has

◀ Giant legs of a colossus of Ramses II, scarred by modern graffiti. *Temple of Ramses II, Abu Simbel.*

two princesses, Meritamun and Henttaui. Ramses has princes Amen(hir)khopshef, Pra-hir-unamef, Merire and Meriatum. The inscriptions on the buttresses inform the world that "Ramses made this temple in the form of an excavation in the hill as an eternal work in the land of Tasetin and nothing like it has been made before".

On the left-hand side of the entrance we see Ramses before Hathor of Abshek, to whom the temple is dedicated, and on the right Nefertary before Isis. Inside the hall the ceiling is supported by six pillars decorated in front with Hathor heads which give the temple a feminine quality always associated with Nefertary. On the walls immediately inside the hall Ramses, as usual, is smiting the enemy—on the right hand a Libyan before Re-Horakhty, and on the left a Negro before Amen-Re.

On the right wall the king stands before Ptah, worships Harsephes and makes libation before Re-Horakhty, whilst the queen stands before Hathor. On the opposite or south wall Ramses stands before Hathor and between Seth of Ombos and Horus. The queen worships Anukis and the king Amen-Re. So far, the king is scoring two to one, but Nefertary gets the whole of the rear wall to herself, with Hathor and Mut. Before we enter the sanctuary we pass through the antechamber to the right of the entrance. There the king and queen are shown before Hathor, and on the left the queen appears between Hathor and Isis. On the north and south walls Ramses takes over again and we see him before the sacred boat bearing Hathor. On the wall containing the entrance to the sanctuary Ramses appears before Re-Horakhty and Amen-Re.

Inside the sanctuary the work is not so fine. To the right, Ramses stands before his deified self and a deified Nefertary; on the left the queen worships Mut and Hathor. In a niche in the rear wall a statue of Hathor springs from the rock. Beneath her, Ramses claims divine protection. The figures are badly mutilated and it appears that this part of the temple was never completed. Uncarved blank spaces in the walls were left by the masons for doors into side chambers that were never excavated. Perhaps Ramses felt he had done enough to immortalise his favourite wife.

A felucca sails past a deserted village near Aswan. The empty doors and windows stare in lonely silence which is occasionally broken by the barking of abandoned dogs.

Queen's temple at Abu Simbel.

The sun passes its zenith and the statues are overtaken by shadows. Tomorrow the sun god will bathe them once more in golden light as he has done more than a million times in their long history.

As the boats leave the shore the temples merge into the sandstone cliffs until they are no longer visible. It is to be hoped that all this wealth of life and movement will be saved from the rising flood. Ramses and his queen inspire sympathy as well as awe. They were real people, whose weaknesses and love of life we know; they are not deities to the peoples who are trying to save them for posterity—they are human beings, immortalised by a giant creative achievement.

View of the Nile at Aswan from the tomb of the Aga Khan. ▶

4: THE FLOOD

The flood which will result from the building of the High Dam at Aswan created international concern for the preservation of the Nubian and Egyptian monuments. The dam itself rivals the pyramids, and will require 56 million cubic yards of materials, enough to build seventeen pyramids the size of Cheops' great monument at Giza. The ironwork alone would be sufficient to make fifteen Eiffel Towers. Much more important than the size is the greatly increased benefits which will follow the harnessing of the river. For years the flood waters ran to waste in the sea. When the floods were high, twenty times as much water was lost as when they were low. The first dam at Aswan was built by the British in 1898. It was over a mile long, 150 feet high and 100 feet thick at the base. When the sluice gates were closed in winter, it flooded the Nile back to the Sudanese frontier over 160 miles away. The High Dam can store the water over several years and release it as required. This will enable five million acres in the Sudan and two million acres in Egypt to be brought under cultivation. The water table in the surrounding area will be raised so that distant oases will become larger and more fertile. The permanent lake formed will cover just under 2,000 square miles. It will be 300 miles long with an

◀ Façade of the temple of Ramses II. Salvage operations begin. Two seated colossi of the king flank the entrance. Above is a statue of Re-Horakhty, falcon-headed god of the horizon. Along the cornice are seated a row of baboons. They were sacred to Thoth, god of Wisdom.　*Façade of the temple of Ramses II, Abu Simbel.*

Work on the High Dam continues round the clock.

average width of six miles and will enormously facilitate navigation. It will also provide for expansion of the fishing industry. America and Britain considered participating in the project but withdrew in 1956. The opportunity (with its attendant propaganda advantages) of making this enormous contribution to the essential economy of Egypt was left to the Russians. They provided technical assistance, personnel and financial aid in the form of a direct loan. The increase in the national income from agricultural and industrial development is expected to be such that both the loan and the interest on it may be repaid within three years of the completion of the Dam.

When finished the Sadd el-Aali, as the dam is called in Arabic, will measure 4,000 yards long, with a width of 1,070 yards at its base and 45 yards at its crest. The height will be 120 yards. The layout of the dam is fairly simple. Through the east bank a deep diversion channel 2,100 yards long, 44 yards wide and 90 yards deep, has been cut in the solid rock. This leads to six tunnels 16 yards in diameter and 260 yards long. These tunnels will pass 14,000 cubic yards of water a second to the biggest hydro-electric power station in the world and thence to the irrigation of the land, both old and reclaimed. It is estimated that it will produce 10,000 million KW hours, or double the present supply, at economic rates. The old Commander of the Inundation would need all his powers to calculate the taxes that will ensue from this massive step towards industrialisation. To force the Nile through the canal a small coffer dam has been built upstream and a similar dam will be built downstream to prevent the river from flowing back into the area where the High Dam will be built. Although these dams are referred to as small, they are higher than the old British dam. On 14th May, 1964, President Gamal Abdel Nasser and Mr. Khrushchev, amidst a cheering crowd of celebrities and workers, exploded the charge that breached the sand barrier at the entrance to the canal and the course of the river was changed for the first time in its long history.

The area between the two coffer dams will be covered with layers of compacted dune sand to a depth of 27 yards. Here the main dam will be built of rock partly provided by the debris from the canal and tunnels. This rock-fill will have an impervious clay core, and a vertical curtain of cement will descend from it into the porous bed of the river to a depth of 230 yards—until it hits natural bedrock and seals off any seepage. Building the dam, like the pyramids, is a question of moving a great deal of heavy material, and the modern Egyptian worker has proved himself as adept as his ancient brother at this gigantic task. Unlike his ancestors, however, the new worker lives in air-conditioned flats and enjoys the free use of excellent clubs and swimming pools, cinema and television. Music from the High Dam's own radio station is on tap for the 30,000 Egyptian and 1,700 Russian workers. They certainly deserve these amenities, for work goes on in an inferno of dust, sweat and noise twenty-four hours a day, seven days a week. Right round the clock the big 25-ton trucks with Rolls-Royce engines are driven at breakneck speed, taking loads of granite from the blasting area to tip them into dumping barges. The barges are hauled into position by tugs and drop their 500-ton cargoes by means of mechanically opening bottoms on to the site. At night the scene is ablaze with lights and looks more like an inferno than ever, swirling clouds of dust and smoke following the roaring trucks and explosions. A monstrous clanging of riveting and hammering continually assails the ears. Through all the uproar one can sense the unmistakable enthusiasm of the workers, for this is something that they really believe in, something that is going to precipitate their country into the twentieth century. To set against the obvious gains one must admit the displacement of 52,000 people from the little villages bordering the Nile which are to be flooded, and the total or partial submerging of a large number of monuments, temples, tombs, fortresses and other relics of the greatest historical and artistic value. The most important of these are the rock temples at Abu Simbel.

The entrance to the six tunnels which will carry water to the power house of Aswan. ▶

Overleaf, left: The sand barrier holding back the waters of the Nile.
Overleaf, right: Blocking the old river bed to force the waters to flow through the new channel.

144

Nefertary and Ramses II with two of their children, princesses Meritamun and Henttaui, who stand dwarfed beneath the figure of their mother on the façade of the Queen's Temple at Abu Simbel. The inscription between the colossi gives the titles of the Queen.

◀ Thousands of lamps turn night into day as work proceeds ahead of schedule.

Faced with this problem, on April 6th, 1959, the government of the U.A.R. asked the Director-General of the United Nations Educational, Scientific and Cultural Organisation for assistance in appealing for international action to safeguard the threatened treasures. The Executive Board of Unesco stated: "As the preservation of the cultural heritage of mankind is one of the Organisation's main tasks under its constitution, it is the Organisation's duty to grant the governments of the U.A.R. and Sudan the assistance they ask for, so as to prevent the irreparable loss to mankind which would result if such priceless monuments and sites were submerged." Following Unesco's enthusiastic support, scientific and technical teams from the Centre de Documentation sur L'Ancienne Egypte at Cairo and large numbers of expert Egyptologists from other countries started to collect all the data possible. Some idea of the world's concern for its cultural heritage may be gained by the hundreds of schemes for saving the temples which poured into the U.A.R. and Unesco. The problem of saving Abu Simbel was complicated by the fact that the temples, being hollowed out of rock, could not be dismantled. There are some twenty-three important monuments in the area to be flooded, but as they are built of blocks of stone it is possible to take them down and rebuild them in a safe place. This has already been most excellently carried out in the case of the temple of Kalabsha, which a German-Egyptian team moved stone by stone to a new site overlooking the cause of it all—the High Dam. The cost of this operation, some half a million pounds, was met by the German government, and the result is well worth the time and money spent. The stones still bear the lines and numbers showing exactly where each must go and no line is even a fraction out of true.

Out of the numerous projects for saving the Abu Simbel monuments the first to be accepted for consideration was the Italian plan. This entailed cutting away the rocks around each temple and encasing them in a reinforced concrete box. Once safely protected by the box the whole structure, including the temples, would be jacked up by 650 synchronised jacks, a sixteenth of an inch at a time. When the jacks were fully extended, prefabricated concrete pillars would be placed under the box and the jacks moved to complete another cycle, raising the box to the next stage. The immensity of this operation is apparent when one realises that the weight of the large temple with its box would be 250,000 tons—three times the weight of the *Queen Elizabeth*. The cost, too, would be enormous—66 million dollars.

The French scheme was even more costly—82 million dollars. This consisted of building a dam, 75 yards high and 1,600 yards long, which would encircle the temples and join the river bank. It would maintain a small sheet of water in front of the temples at the present level so that much of the original beauty of the situation would be preserved. Of course, the very height of the dam would obstruct the early sunrise and the inner sanctuary would never again receive its baptism of light.

Arab workmen watch the long pipelines discharging a mixture of dune sand and water to fill in the dam area.

A Bedouin watches the activities on the site of the power station of the High Dam.

Some idea of the proportions of this task may be gained from the ancillary and preparatory works:

> a town for 3,000 people;
> an airport;
> two harbours, one at High Dam and one at Abu Simbel;
> 22 miles of road.

In addition to this, equipment would be needed to move 26 million cubic yards of materials into position and to pump out unwanted water. The final result would look well, as can be seen from the perspective sketch. The Nile at Abu Simbel is

Egyptologists' camp beside a site on the river between Aswan and Abu Simbel.

over half a mile in width and the arc of the dam would be 325 yards from the temples, and the places where it joined the bank of the river would be 1,100 yards apart, so that the original prospect would be preserved.

Among the plans was one submitted by the author of this book. The idea was simply to leave the temples in their beautiful setting but surround them with a thin membrane dam, using filters which would only allow clean water next to the temples, keeping out the muddy deposits of the Nile. The pressure being equal on both sides of the membrane would mean that only a very light structure would be needed. Underwater passages with windows and floodlights would enable visitors to see the beauties of the temples, crystal clear under water as if they were in an aquarium. Chemicals added to the filtered water would harden and petrify the soft sandstone, which would thus be preserved forever. Sandstorms could not erode the carvings as they have done with the colossi of Memnon.

This scheme had certain advantages, the greatest, possibly, being that there was no expense involved in keeping the water out and the whole operation, including air-conditioning, lifts, restaurant and equipment, would cost £2,300,000. It would also be practical to visit the temples in comfort at any time of the year, and the rising sun could be artificially simulated as frequently as desired. On top of this the appeal of the drowned temples would prove a permanent tourist attraction and the cost of admission would more than cover the upkeep. The plan had an excellent international press and was considered to be the most sophisticated idea to come forward, but the committee felt that the temples would be safer on dry land, and so the Swedish scheme received their blessing and was adopted.

This plan was to cut the temples up into conveniently sized blocks and to re-erect them on a suitable site at the top of the cliff. This rather drastic treatment had certain dangers, chiefly that the friable sandstone might disintegrate during the

◀ Construction work on the hydro-electric plant. Note how the rock has been blasted out in huge steps.

Min being worshipped by Ramses, on one of the huge pillars of the great hall at Karnak.

View from the temple of Queen Nefertary towards that of Ramses II at Abu Simbel. ▶

Overleaf, left: Entrance to the sarcophagus-chamber of Queen Nefertary. Maet, goddess of Truth, spreads her wings across the lintel. The name and titles of the Queen are written on the door jambs: "Great Royal Wife, Mistress of the Two Lands (Upper and Lower Egypt), Nefertary".
Tomb of Nefertary, Thebes, Luxor.

Overleaf, right: The goddess Hathor, wearing the sign of a falcon on a perch, meaning the "west" (where the dead are buried). She holds by the arm Re-Horakhty, the falcon-headed god of the horizon.
Tomb of Nefertary.

Hathor-headed pillars in the temple of Nefertary.

◀ A side room in the tomb of Queen Nefertary. On the left is Osiris, his flesh painted green, the colour of resurrection. In front of him, on a pedestal, stand the Four Sons of Horus, protectors of the viscera of a dead person. On the right of the central fan sits Atum, Heliopolitan god of Creation. The Queen (not visible) is making burnt offerings to both gods. *Thebes, Luxor.*

sawing up process, but many sample borings have been taken and the Swedish engineers have checked and rechecked the internal stresses and consistencies of the rocks. The plan will require a coffer dam to keep the Nile out while the cutting up takes place. The cost of the scheme will be £14 million.

On the golden sand before the temples there now stands a large yellow crane surrounded by hundreds of bright-red drums of fuel. Beyond the crane lie piles of long steel girders. Down the river comes a stream of barges carrying stores and equipment. A hydrofoil skims over the Nile at forty miles an hour, stopping abruptly to unload fifty tourists who will have a brief hour to pay homage to the temples. They have come from all parts of the world for this wonderful moment and it is evident from their expressions that they think their long journeys well worth the trouble and expense.

Another ship, the *Dolphin*, built at Alexandria, is fitted out like an aircraft. With air-conditioning and picture windows, she carries over a hundred visitors at 20 miles an hour. More sedately comes an old warrior with paddle wheels. It takes two days for the trip from Aswan, but provides comfortable cabins and dressing for dinner—a tribute to the more leisurely days when the visitor spent a large part of the winter in Egypt. The stream of tourists seems never-ending; the imagination of the world has been captured.

High above the colossi the dog-headed apes scan the horizon as they have done since they were carved 1,257 years before the birth of Christ. Below them a German television crew set up their cameras. The Reverend James Baikie may rest in peace. For here the nations are collectively undertaking the largest salvage operation since the beginning of the world. The motives are entirely non-political, the atmosphere is one of peaceful co-operation to save a part of the cultural heritage of mankind. How Ramses would have relished this situation . . . Hydrofoils, air-conditioned ships, and people from the far corners of the earth, all coming to pay homage to his vast memorial.

In a sense, he does indeed live again.

Queen Nefertary standing beside a table of offerings which includes loaves of bread, a jar of wine, a haunch of meat and baskets of grapes. She holds out two vases to Hathor (not visible). *Tomb of Nefertary.*

5: MANY TREASURES

Many treasures of the world have vanished forever. Of the Seven Wonders, only one has survived—the Pyramids, and few people could name the remaining six: the Gardens of Semiramis at Babylon; the Statue of Zeus at Olympia; the Temple of Artemis at Ephesus; the Mausoleum at Halicarnassus; the Colossus of Rhodes; and the Pharos of Alexandria. We know from the records of Antipator of Sidon that these monuments were in existence as recently as 200 B.C. Six of the Wonders have vanished completely, but on the way to Cairo the Nile flows past many priceless monuments that still remain.

Foreigners have often thought that these treasures would be safer if removed to their own lands. The obelisks of Egypt have received a lot of this kind of attention. These slim tapering needles covered with historical script were consecrated to the sun god, Amen-Re. Their pyramidal tips were plated with electrum, a mixture of gold and silver which was designed to reflect the light of the sun into the temple and to tell the passing hours. The one in Piazza di San Pietro in Rome still serves this purpose, although the addition of a cross on the apex was an eventuality that the ancient Egyptians would scarcely have foreseen.

Most of the obelisks were cut from the red granite of the quarries at Aswan. In fact, one still remains three-quarters cut, with its lower side attached to the living rock. This giant is 42 metres long and weighs 1,168 tons. It illustrates the method

164

Staring at each other throughout eternity, two heads form stoppers for the canopic jars holding the liver and lungs of a mummy. The more perishable organs were removed before embalmment. *Cairo Museum.*

used by the ancient masons. The rough shape of the obelisk was cut out by pounding the hard granite with balls of green dolerite, five to twelve inches in diameter, an excessively tough stone. This broke a channel round the object. To separate the mass from the mother rock, slots were cut with copper chisels, and wedges of sycamore hammered home and then soaked with water. The resulting swelling of the wood split the rock along the line chosen by the masons. Little did the builders think that their handiwork would travel all over the world.

Rome has seven, London one, Constantinople two, Florence two, Washington one, New York one, and there are four in France, the most famous of which is that of Ramses II which graces the Place de la Concorde. It was given by Mohammed

Ali to Louis Philippe of France in exchange for the large clock now in the Citadel in Cairo. On its side is written: "Ramses, the powerful and the strong, conqueror of all foreign peoples, master of all crown bearers, Ramses who fought the millions, who bids the whole world to subdue itself to his power upon the wish of his father Amun the Great."

At Aswan, 166 miles north of Abu Simbel, the island of Elephantine marks the first cataract and its Nilometer bears the flood marks of the Nile, used to calculate the rate of taxes. Beyond the island on top of a hill stands the beautiful mausoleum of the Aga Khan, looking out over the view he loved so much, the water flowing swiftly between the great black rocks with the white-sailed feluccas moving gracefully against the dusky violet of the distant hills.

North of Aswan lie the new settlements for the displaced peoples of Abu Simbel and of the whole flood area. The houses are built in orderly rows, very different from the deserted villages which they replace. At first the newcomers will miss their old houses beside the sandy beaches with the great river gliding past.

A herdsman watches over his cattle in one of the tombs of the nobles. Possibly the tomb of Nebamun 1450 B.C.

Queen Nefertary, wife of Ramses II, offering the symbol for "clothing" to Ptah, Memphite god of creation, who holds a sceptre in the form of a *djed*-column, surmounted by the signs for "power" and "eternity". The queen wears a diaphanous linen robe tied with a sash. The vulture-headdress, like a golden bird seated upon her head, is an emblem of royalty; it is surmounted by the divine feathers of Amun.   *Tomb of Nefertary*.

But to compensate for that they will have an easier life and a higher standard of living. Thirty-two new villages have been built lying in the 34,000 acres of fertile land that has been specially prepared for irrigation and cultivation. Each village is complete with a school, medical centre, mosque, market, small industries and a social centre. The 25,000 new houses are stone built and contain two, three or four rooms, with a kitchen and lavatory. There is also a yard and a place to keep

167

domestic animals and birds. Each house will have one door for the guests and one door for the house, corresponding with our front and back doors.

The resettlement is done village by village, so that the communities remain the same and neighbours will continue to be neighbours, with the life of the village disturbed as little as possible.

At Luxor, 130 miles beyond Aswan, lies the Valley of the Kings. The first tomb inside the main gateway is that of Ramses II. Naturally enough, he chose the best site for himself. Inside the tomb is a steep rubble-filled passage with wooden timbers supporting the roof. Some of the timbers do not quite reach the roof. The tomb is dangerous and has been shut for many years. The passage continues a long way down and leads to a large underground chamber, also blocked with falls of rock and debris. Although there is a feeling of insecurity, it is not an eerie sensation, nor is there an "atmosphere of death". Indeed there is nothing fearsome about any of the tombs of Ancient Egypt. Leading from the main chamber is a small hole which leads into another chamber but here, too, everything is choked with rubbish. The archaeologist who discovered this tomb must have been very disappointed to find it empty. In fact the royal mummy was first moved as long ago as 973 B.C., when it was placed in a new coffin and put in the tomb of Queen Inhapi.

Nearby is the house where Howard Carter lived when he opened the tomb of Tutankhamen on 22nd November, 1922. The rooms surrounded a central hall

Colossal head of Ramses II in the Temple of Luxor. He is wearing the double crown and the Uraeus of the ▶
Cobra Goddess, Wadjyt.

Overleaf, left: Queen Nefertary, wearing a gold collar over her fine linen robe and the gold vulture-headdress, is led by Isis. The Queen's name is written in the cartouche between the two figures.
Tomb of Nefertary.

Overleaf, right: Nephthys and Isis either side of Re, the sun god, who wears the ram's head of Khnum, god of Elephantine.
Tomb of Nefertary.

Left and above: An Egyptian artist reproduces the ancient colouring on plaster casts taken from the Queen's Temple at Abu Simbel. It shows the Queen between Hathor and Isis.

with a domed roof in which a series of ventilators provide a breeze from whichever direction the wind may come.

The tomb of Queen Nefertary is near by in the Valley of the Tombs of the Queens. It lies in the first position to the right like that of her husband.

The name Nefertary means "Beautiful Companion", and this she certainly must have been to have retained the affections of her husband, with his multitudes of wives and concubines. She was married to Ramses before he became a Pharaoh, and he commemorated his love for her on many of his monuments as well as having

Queen Nefertary, represented as Osiris, the god of the dead and of resurrection, whose mummified form was copied by the embalmers in order to ensure that the deceased would come to life again. She is lying on a bier decorated with a lion's head, tail and legs, over which is draped a coloured canopy. The kites either end of the bier represent the goddesses Isis (*right*) and Nephthys, who traditionally guarded a dead person. The benu-bird, a heron, another symbol of resurrection, stands behind Nephthys.

Tomb of Nefertary, Valley of the Queens, Luxor.

the temple at Abu Simbel dedicated to her—a rare honour indeed. The date of her death and the whereabouts of her mummy are still unknown.

The entrance to Nefertary's tomb leads to a small room which has a ledge running along the left and rear walls, probably for the reception of offerings. The white stucco walls are covered with gay, colourful paintings of the gods and

174

Interior of the tomb of Queen Nefertary at Thebes. The queens and princesses (and some princes) were buried in a separate valley from the kings on the west bank of the Nile directly opposite the temple of Luxor. The paintings in the tomb of Nefertary are remarkably beautiful, but unfortunately damp is now attacking the walls and much may soon be lost. *Pillar on the left:* a figure of the priest Iunmutef, wearing a panther skin. *Pillar facing:* a *djed*-column—a symbol of Osiris, god of the dead.　　　*Valley of the Queens, Luxor.*

175

goddesses, together with picture writing from the Book of the Dead. The outline of the paintings is clear-cut and decisive and the effect is full of life and gaiety. The atmosphere is feminine and there is a feeling that the perfume Nefertary used would be appropriate here, but no scent or incense pervades the cool air in the tomb.

On the wall on the right of the entrance the queen worships Osiris; on the left her Ka plays a game, and, farther on, adores the rising sun which appears between two lions, Yesterday and Tomorrow. The mural continues with a blue crane and two hawks representing Isis and Nephthys watching the bier of Osiris, the symbol of resurrection. Here in the wall a doorway leads down a steep stairway to the burial hall. Above the doorway are the four sons of Horus—Imseti (human-headed), Hapi (ape-headed), Duamutef (jackal-headed), and Qebehsenuef (falcon-headed)—who are married to the four goddesses of the canopic jars. On either side of the stairway the long triangles formed by the sloping roof are filled with pictures which adorn the space available with great elegance. On the right the queen makes an offering to Hathor, who sits on a throne with Selqet behind her. On the opposite triangle she offers two bowls of wine to Isis, behind whom sits Nephthys. In the narrowest part of the triangles Maet sits with her wings before her.

The bottom of the stairs leads into the burial hall, the roof of which is supported by four square pillars, with a sunken area between them where once stood the sarcophagus. Here the work has been damaged by a moist, salty exudate coming through the plaster, and because of this the tomb has not been opened for many years. It is to be hoped that some remedy will be found for this before it attacks the work in the upper chambers. The sanctuary of the tomb is in the rear wall and is sadly spoilt; only fragments of the painting can be seen.

Path outside the tomb of Ramses II in the Valley of the Kings, where most of the great rulers of the New King-dom were buried, in tombs tunnelled into the cliffs. The necropolis was known to the ancient Egyptians as the "Place of Truth"—its Arabic name means "Gates of the Kings". *Thebes, Luxor.*

On the way out to the left is a side chamber with charming paintings of the queen adoring the seven sacred cattle, the bull and the four steering oars of the sky. On the rear wall she presents offerings to Osiris and to Atum.

Four hundred and twenty miles father north, Cairo, the largest city in Africa, bustles with the life of modern Egypt. In the centre of its swirling traffic and teeming population stands its famous museum dedicated to its founder Auguste Mariette, the great Frenchman responsible for stopping the activities of unauthorised excavators, who were wastefully pillaging the tombs and selling the antiquities abroad. In the heart of this fabulous treasure house, surrounded by the priceless works of the past, rests the mummy of Ramses II. His wanderings end in a setting that even he could hardly have bettered. Here in a plain wooden coffin beneath protecting glass lies the great Pharaoh. The mummy is covered with a yellowing cloth which reveals the left hand raised in its final gesture. Around him the other royal mummies, including his son, lie at peace. Ramses' head is uncovered and well poised on the slender neck. The chin and mouth are firm, the nose high-arched and commanding; the eyes, deep in their sockets, are closed and slanting slightly upwards, giving a certain shrewdness to the face. Locks of light brown hair from the back of the head lie on the pillow. The ears are large and the jawbones jut out. It is a strong, arrogant face, showing none of the senility of a man reputed to be nearly a century old when he died. His many moves do not appear to have left any scars, but the light-brown skin, with here and there darker traces of preservative, has weathered almost 33 centuries. People from all parts of the world come to pay homage to him and to the concept that the dead may live again.

Entrance of the tomb of Ramses II in the Valley of the Kings. After the complicated funeral rites, the tomb and its rich contents were sealed up and all trace of its whereabouts removed, in the hope that robbers would not come and despoil the tomb. These efforts were in vain—even the body of the king himself was rifled for the costly jewels and amulets wound in with the mummy wrappings. *Thebes, Luxor.*

APPENDICES

SCHEMES FOR SAVING THE TEMPLES

1. THE SWEDISH SCHEME

In the foreground is a small dam to keep the rising waters at bay until the temples are cut into blocks and removed to their new sites, the crescent-shaped positions which can be seen in the background. The rock above the temples has been partly removed prior to the cutting of the blocks. On top of the dam is the roadway by which they will be taken to the new position. On the left, in the background, is a group of blocks which have already been cut out. The ceiling portions will be among the first to be removed as they will be the last to be used when the temples are rebuilt. The whole process of rebuilding will take between two and three years. During this time the blocks will be protected by plastic foam.

181

2. THE FRENCH SCHEME

This huge dam is approximately 300 feet high and a mile long and holds back the new high level waters of the Nile. Roads lead down in sweeping curves to the temples still in their original setting, fronted by a small lake whose surface is kept at the old level of the river.

3. THE ITALIAN SCHEME

Part of the rock has been cut away and the temples enclosed in huge concrete boxes heavily reinforced with steel. Beneath the boxes 650 synchronised jacks are ready to raise the temples a sixteenth of an inch at a time. When the jacks are fully extended, concrete pillars are placed under the boxes and the operation repeated until the temples are raised above the danger line.

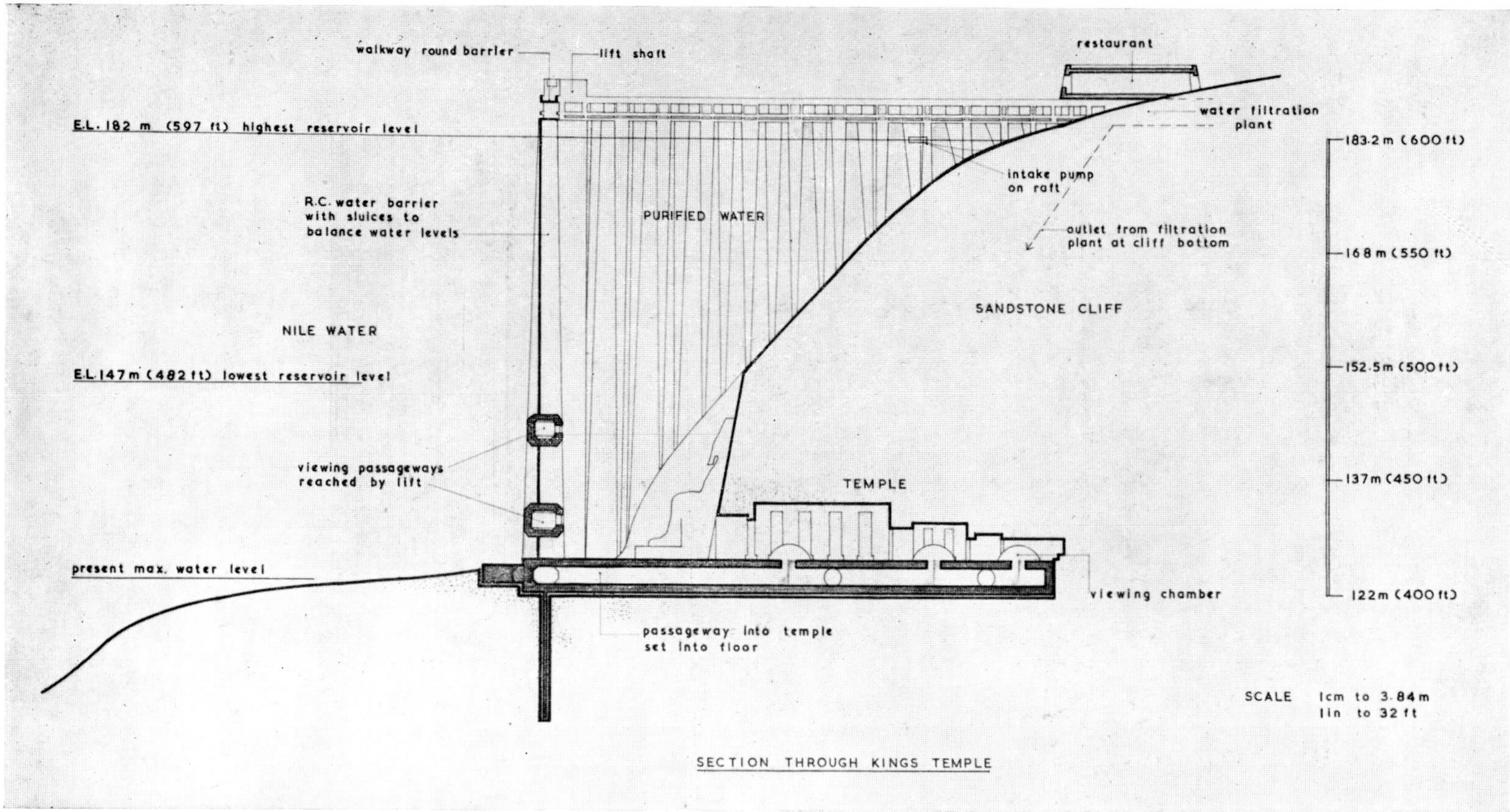
walkway round barrier
lift shaft
restaurant
E.L. 182 m (597 ft) highest reservoir level
water filtration plant
183.2 m (600 ft)
intake pump on raft
R.C. water barrier with sluices to balance water levels
PURIFIED WATER
outlet from filtration plant at cliff bottom
168 m (550 ft)
SANDSTONE CLIFF
NILE WATER
E.L. 147 m (482 ft) lowest reservoir level
152.5 m (500 ft)
viewing passageways reached by lift
TEMPLE
137 m (450 ft)
present max. water level
viewing chamber
122 m (400 ft)
passageway into temple set into floor
SCALE 1cm to 3.84m
1in to 32 ft
SECTION THROUGH KINGS TEMPLE

4. THE AUTHOR'S SCHEME

In this cross section the Great Temple is seen submerged in clear water. The muddy waters of the Nile are kept out by a membrane dam a foot thick. It does not have to be heavily constructed as the pressure of water on either side always remains the same. Running through the dam are two passages at different levels. These contain reinforced glass windows through which the colossi can be seen from various angles. Powerful electric lights reproduce the rising and setting of the sun. Further passages lead beneath the temple floors and emerge into reinforced glass chambers from which the interiors of the temples can be examined. The water is constantly filtered and supplied with chemicals to ensure the preservation of the sandstone.

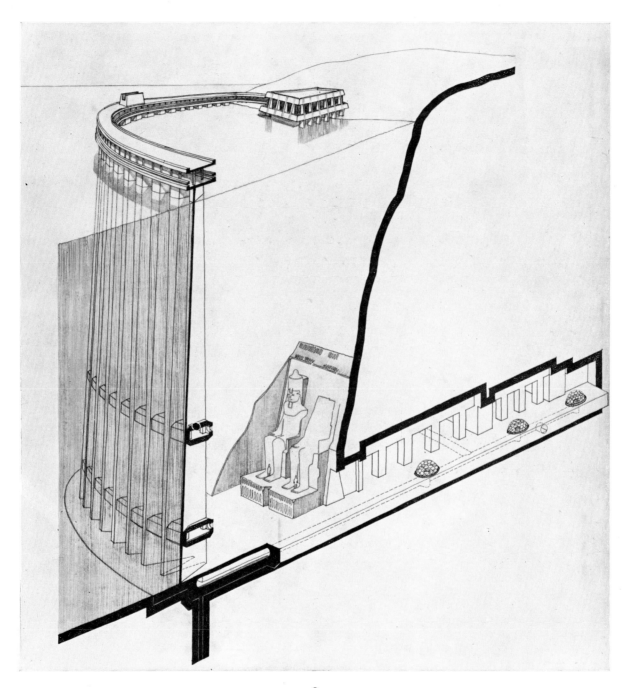

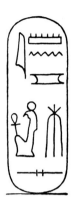

THE NAMES OF RAMSES II

Ramses II, like most Egyptian kings, possessed a long series of names and epithets of which two had special importance. These were the names placed inside cartouches —ovals which originally represented loops of rope with ties, probably signifying in a graphic manner that the king ruled all "which the sun encircled". The first cartouche of Ramses II, containing a name which is sometimes called the prenomen, can be seen in a good example on page 169: . In translation this name reads *One powerful of Truth is Re, he whom Re has chosen*; in Egyptian it may have sounded something like Usimare-Sotpenre. It will be noted that the name is here shown in reverse of the form found on the arm of the king on pages 78 and 84. There is no significance in this change, for Egyptian texts could be written monumentally from left to right, or from right to left, and horizontally or vertically. Here the names are written to be read from left to right in order to fit in with the direction of the English text. The breakdown of the signs in this first name is as follows: ⊙, the sun-disc, representing the god Re; , a ritual staff with a jackal-head, having the phonetic value W + S + R, a verb meaning "be powerful"; , a figure of Maet, the goddess of Truth; ⊙, again the sun-disc; , an adze with block of wood, with the phonetic value S + T + P, a verb meaning "choose", which, in combination with the sign ⌇⌇⌇ (a ripple of water, of phonetic value N), represents here a special verbal form. The precedence given to the sign

186

⊙ in both parts of the name is a graphic peculiarity of hieroglyphic writing which required that prominence be given to divine names in certain contexts.

On the front cover of this book can be seen the second cartouche of Ramses II, containing again a double name, often called the nomen: . It can be translated *One beloved of Amun, one born of Re*—in Egyptian pronounced possibly Miamun-Ramessu. The signs of which the name is composed are the following: first, three signs 'spelling' out the name of the god Amun— , the reed-leaf, with a phonetic value close to A; , a gaming-board with pieces in position, having the phonetic value M + N; and the water-sign , of phonetic value N, here used to complement the N implicit in ; then comes , an irrigation channel of phonetic value M + R, here representing a form of the verb "love". The second part of the name, which can be seen to be the origin of Ramses, consists of , a seated divine falcon with a sun-disc on its head, representing Re; , three foxes' skins tied together, of phonetic value M + S, here being a form of the verb "bear"; , a door-bolt, with value S, representing a pronominal form.

The order and choice of signs used in writing these names are capable of great variation; thus the forms of the names discussed here represent only one set of possibilities.

We are indebted to Mr. T. G. H. James, the Assistant Keeper of the department of Egyptian Antiquities, British Museum, for the above information.

187

CHRONOLOGICAL TABLE

Including the names of the principal kings

Early Dynastic Period

       First Dynasty (c. 3100–2890 B.C.)

Narmer (Menes)   Den

Aha   Semerkhet

Djer   Qaa

       Second Dynasty (c. 2890–2686 B.C.)

Hotepsekhemwy   Peribsen

Nynetjer   Khasekhemwy

Old Kingdom

       Third Dynasty (c. 2686–2613 B.C.)

Sanakhte   Sekhemkhet

Djoser (Zoser)   Huni

       Fourth Dynasty (c. 2613–2494 B.C.)

Sneferu   Chephren

Cheops   Mycerinus

       Fifth Dynasty (c. 2494–2345 B.C.)

Userkaf   Nyuserre

Sahure   Unas

       Sixth Dynasty (c. 2345–2181 B.C.)

Teti   Merenre

Pepi I   Pepi II

First Intermediate Period

A time of political instability lasting from about 2181 B.C. to about 2133 B.C., including the Seventh to Tenth Dynasties, the order and names of whose kings are not fully established.

Middle Kingdom

       Eleventh Dynasty (c. 2133–1991 B.C.)

Mentuhotpe I   Mentuhotpe II–IV

Inyotef I–III

       Twelfth Dynasty (c. 1991–1786 B.C.)

Ammenemes I, 1991–1962 B.C.   Sesostris III, 1878–1843 B.C.

Sesostris I, 1971–1928 B.C.   Ammenemes III, 1842–1797 B.C.

       Thirteenth Dynasty (c. 1786–1633 B.C.)

Sebekhotpe III   Neferhotep

Second Intermediate Period

A further time of political instability during which Egypt was ruled in part by the Asiatic Hyksos. The Fourteenth and Sixteenth Dynasties are particularly shadowy, the former consisting of native rulers, and the latter of minor Hyksos.

       Fifteenth (Hyksos) Dynasty (c. 1674–1567 B.C.)

Sheshi   Apophis I

Khyan   Apophis II

Seventeenth Dynasty (c. 1650–1567 B.C.)

Seqenenre   Kamose

New Kingdom

Eighteenth Dynasty (c. 1567–1320 B.C.)

Amosis, 1570–
1546 B.C.

Amenophis I, 1546–
1526 B.C.

Tuthmosis I, 1525–
1512 B.C.

Tuthmosis II, 1512–
1504 B.C.

Hatshepsut, 1503–
1482 B.C.

Tuthmosis III, 1504–
1450 B.C.

Amenophis II, 1450–
1425 B.C.

Tuthmosis IV, 1425–
1417 B.C.

Amenophis III, 1417–
1379 B.C.

Akhenaten, 1379–
1362 B.C.

Smenkhkare, 1364–
1361 B.C.

Tutankhamen, 1361–
1352 B.C.

Ay, 1352–1348 B.C.

Horemheb, 1348–
1320 B.C.

Nineteenth Dynasty (c. 1320–1200 B.C.)

Ramses I, 1320–1318
B.C.

Seti I, 1318–1304 B.C.

Ramses II, 1304–
1237 B.C.

Merneptah, 1236–1223
B.C.

Amenmesses, 1222–
1217 B.C.

Seti II, 1216–1210 B.C.

Twentieth Dynasty (c. 1200–1085 B.C.)

Sethnakhte, 1200–
1198 B.C.

Ramses III, 1198–
1166 B.C.

Ramses IV–XI, 1166–
1085 B.C.

Late New Kingdom

From the Twenty-first to the beginning of the Twenty-fifth Dynasties (*c.* 1085–750 B.C.), Egypt was in political decline. The Twenty-fourth Dynasty was concurrent with the beginning of the Twenty-fifth Dynasty.

Late Period

Twenty-fifth Dynasty (c. 750–656 B.C.)

Piankhi, 750–716 B.C.   Taharqa, 689–664 B.C.

Shabaka, 716–695 B.C.

Twenty-sixth Dynasty (c. 664–525 B.C.)

Psammetichus I, 664–
610 B.C.

Apries, 589–570 B.C.

Necho II, 610–595 B.C.   Amasis, 570–526 B.C.

The Twenty-seventh Dynasty consisted of Assyrian conquering kings, and the Twenty-eighth–Thirtieth Dynasties of the last native Egyptian rulers. In 332 B.C. Alexander the Great conquered Egypt, and thereafter the land was ruled first by Macedonian Greeks (the Ptolemies) and then as part of the Roman Empire.

We are indebted to Mr. T. G. H. James also for the above Chronological Table.

INDEX

The bold figures refer to illustrations

191